the
IMMORALITY
of
PROMISING

the
IMMORALITY
of
PROMISING

RICHARD M. FOX
and
JOSEPH P. DeMARCO

Humanity
Books

an imprint of Prometheus Books
59 John Glenn Drive, Amherst, New York 14228-2197

Published 2001 by Humanity Books, an imprint of Prometheus Books

Inquiries should be addressed to
Humanity Books
59 John Glenn Drive
Amherst, New York 14228–2197
VOICE: 716–691–0133, ext. 207
FAX: 716–564–2711

04 03 02 01 00   5 4 3 2 1

Library of Congress Cataloging-in-Publication Data

Fox, Richard M., 1931–
    The immorality of promising / Richard M. Fox and Joseph P. DeMarco.
        p. cm.
    Includes bibliographical references and index.
    ISBN 1–57392–864–X (cloth : alk. paper)
    1. Promises. 2. Ethics. I. DeMarco, Joseph P., 1943– II. Title.

BJ1500.P7 F69 2000
170—dc21   00–047207

Printed in the United States of America on acid-free paper

Only what I am always telling you, Crito, nothing very new. Look after yourselves: then anything you do will be of service to me and mine, and to yourselves too, even if at this moment you make no promises to that effect; but if you neglect yourselves, and refuse to follow that path of life which has been traced out in this present conversation and in others that we have had before, then, plentiful and vehement though your present promises may be, all you do will be fruitless.

—Plato
Phaedo

CONTENTS

PREFACE

The idea for this book was born nearly a decade ago when, in a conversation mainly about other things, one of us remarked that there seemed to be something radically wrong with promises. When the point of the remark was explained, the other understood immediately, and we wondered why nobody had ever thought of it before. Well, perhaps someone did, but we were not aware of anyone who, in the long history of philosophy, had explicitly advanced the thesis in print. It appeared to us that all of the major figures in the history of ethical theory and even contemporary writers on the subject were of just the opposite opinion. Some, indeed, have stated flat out that the justification of the practice of promising is beyond question. Others, we knew, recognized that there were problems with promising which they thought they could fix, and still others, we discovered later, actually pointed to the difficulties without drawing from them what we take to be the rather obvious conclusion that promising is immoral.

But philosophers, and perhaps many others as well, are deeply attached to promises and find them hard to give up. In the philosophic community, entire careers and reputations have been built on defending promises, or on assuming their justification, as promising is

9

usually thought to be fundamental to moral life. It dawned on us, naturally, that our position was not likely to win immediate or widespread acceptance. We knew that we would have to defend ourselves on all fronts, against practically every moral theory on the subject. The task before us, we thought, would be something like trying to prove that the emperor is not wearing clothes!

And we were right at least in this, for practically everyone who has read our papers or heard our arguments thinks we are wrong, dead wrong, *obviously* wrong. Although, in our opinion, none has been able to show us wrong, they seem convinced that we must be wrong and that our arguments, therefore, are, or at least should be, easy to defeat. But the rebuttals we have seen and heard all seem to avoid the full thrust of our critique, perhaps because they misunderstand our arguments, or because, as seems likely to us, they do not fully understand their own. That is, our critics have attacked us on one point here and another point there without considering our main argument against them, namely, that their own beliefs about promises do not cohere. Their undying faith in promises, we try to demonstrate, is based upon confusion: on ambiguous and equivocal statements about the meaning and moral force of promises. Yet they appear to be untroubled with ad hoc defenses of their own theories in which they facilely take back with one hand what they give with another.

In presenting our arguments, therefore, we challenge the defenders of promises to give a clear and consistent explanation of their own positions instead of merely claiming, for one isolated reason or another, that our position is untenable. We invite them to *put together* the claims they make, side by side, and show how they can render consistent the various beliefs about promising that we hold are inconsistent. If, for example, promising is an acceptable moral practice, and if promising really creates a moral obligation, we would like to see an explanation of what exactly a promise obligates a person to do and why. We go to great lengths to prove they can't, and we would be happy to hear from anyone who thinks they can. We can be reached by email: j.demarco@popmail.csuohio.edu.

Since this book is built around three previously published articles, one of which bears the same title, we begin with an introductory chapter entitled "A Reply to our Critics." Although it may seem that we are thus placing last things first, we nevertheless felt that we had to meet head on, at the very beginning, the usual sorts of criticism that have been brought against us, to fend off, as it were, premature responses that would cause our readers to turn a deaf ear to our arguments or prevent them from reading the rest of the book. There are, moreover, many other theses advanced than the one indicated by the title, and we wanted to announce some of them up front, lest those who are put off by our major argument fail to notice that our book makes an important contribution to other topics as well. Whether or not promising is immoral, there are still major flaws in the standard, received accounts of the obligation-creating force of promises, the conditions under which promises can justifiably be made, and the reasons why obligations of promise keeping may be said to hold.

The second chapter, entitled "The Incoherence of Received Views," reviews in greater detail the accepted wisdom on promising, pointing exactly where the fundamental problems with promising lie, and demonstrating why various attempts to resolve these issues have failed. Errors arise, for instance, in the very definitions of promising proposed in the literature, some of which mistakenly assert that promising, by definition, creates a moral obligation. Other philosophic difficulties are created by the recognition that the so-called duty of promise keeping is defeasible, which philosophers usually think they can untangle by putting restrictions on promises, or by simply claiming that promise keeping is a prima facie duty. We address these restrictions at several points in the book, attempting to show that promising cannot be saved by appealing to the notion of prima facie duty and that the conditions placed on promising by philosophers simply do not hold.

"Putting Pressure on Promises," the third chapter, is a previously published article that has been modified only slightly for this work. In it we argue that promises are deceptive and misleading partly because of conflicting interpretations of the moral force of promising. We attempt to explain why ordinary promises, generally recognized by philosophers as paradigmatic, suffer from many of the same problems as degenerate promises, or promises which most philosophers would claim are defective. This chapter lays the groundwork for our main argument, in chapter 4, that promising is immoral.

The argument in chapter 4, "The Immorality of Promising," is presented in the form of a dilemma in which the choice of either horn leads to untenable conclusions. Although roughly the first half of this chapter was previously published as a journal article, it has been expanded substantially by including a schematic view of the argument, by blocking attempts to obviate the options we present, and by attacking the idea that the morality of promising can be salvaged by appealing to the popular philosophic doctrine that promise keeping is a prima facie obligation. We also present, at the end of this chapter, two paradoxes of promising which, as far as we know, have been heretofore unnoticed by philosophers.

Chapter 5, "On Making and Keeping Promises," also a published article, shows that the dilemma presented in the previous chapter cannot be resolved by putting restrictions of promise making, as so many philosophers have attempted to do. We take up the conditions placed on promising, one by one, explaining, in the first place, why they are not legitimate restrictions on the validity or justification of promise making, and why, in the second place, such restrictions have nothing to do with the morality of promise keeping. This is just one, yet fundamental, confusion that underlies the belief that promises can be saved from the arguments we bring against them: a confusion that seems to affect practically every philosophic account of the so-called institution of promising.

We address the question of the similarities and differences between promising, and other related acts, such as agreeing and contracting, in a number of places, but we believed it was especially important , for several reasons, to include a chapter on contracts, chapter 6. One of the reasons is that promises have often been confused with contracts, or, more commonly, contracts with promises; we believe that it is important to distinguish the two. We also discovered in our reading of contract law that the law of contract has changed over the years, for many of the same reasons we think that promising itself ought to change, or be eliminated, out of respect for moral rules and principles. That is, we think that promises ought to be curtailed in deference to moral principles and rules in much the same way that contracts are now restricted by legal principles and statutes, wherein the primary concerns of the courts are justice and nonmaleficence and not the mere keeping of a person's word.

Chapter 7, called "Reasonable Reliance," develops our own theory of the duty of promise keeping and defends it against opposing positions. We try to show in this chapter that, among other things, promising is not an obligation-creating act and that the duty to keep a promise, when such a duty exists, does not depend on its being so. We distinguish the assurance given by promises from the obligation to keep promises, because these two aspects of promising are not the same, although they are obviously related and easily conflated. We also establish conditions that must be met in order for a duty of promise keeping to hold, and we also discuss at some length the question of the rights and duties of promisees, as well as those of promisors.

Although chapter 7 completes our argument, we have added a "Concluding Postscript," chapter 8, to draw out what we take to be some of the implications of our position. Among these is the important point that, if we are correct, promising can no longer be used as a paradigm for illustrating the nature of moral obligation or as a test of the comprehensiveness or consistency of moral theory. It also cannot be used, as in social contract theory, as a foundation for the creation of moral rules. However, the implications for moral philosophy aside, promising should not be used as a refuge for scoundrels who uphold a philosophy of trust, or loyalty, above principles of justice and nonmaleficence. That is, promising is immoral.

We wish to thank the editors of the following journals for their permission to use materials from our previously published articles: the *Journal of Value Inquiry* for "The Immorality of Promising," the *Southern Journal of Philosophy* for "Putting Pressure on Promises," and the *Journal of Applied Ethics* for "On Making and Keeping Promises."

We dedicate this book to our wives, Patricia A. Fox and Bonnie S. DeMarco.

one

INTRODUCTION

A Reply to Our Critics

Promise: A declaration assuring that one will or will not do something.[1]

Promise: A declaration or assurance made to another person with respect to the future, stating that one will do, or refrain from, some specified act, or that one will give or bestow some specified thing.[2]

Our thesis that promising is immoral may seem rather shocking, although it is certainly not our intention to shock. We are aware, of course, that our position appears to be counterintuitive and that it opposes both popular and academic views on the subject. Almost no one who has read our papers on this topic, or who has heard our arguments, agrees with us. Indeed, most seem to think that refutation of our position is easy. But we maintain nevertheless that it is *they* and not we who are wrong, and we attempt to show this by the arguments in this book.

The argument we present is multifaceted and hence somewhat subtle and complex. The general form of it is simple enough, but it becomes more complicated as we find it necessary to defend our premises against those who make contrary assumptions, or against those who believe they can reconcile assumptions which, we hold, are inconsistent.

Our opponents, of course, are not only contemporary philosophers who ascribe to competing theories of promising. Our position seems to contradict common sense and a rather long and hallowed tradition in philosophy, both of which regard promise making and promise keeping as linchpins of moral life. There has been widespread acceptance of the belief that persons have a special moral obligation to keep promises, and a number of ethical theorists have looked upon promise keeping as a paradigm of moral obligation—even as the very basis of moral obligation itself!

If not always by actual assertion, then by implication at least, many moral philosophers have held the view that the making of promises is not only good but necessary to morality. Promising is regularly thought to be the foundation of contract and, in social contract theories, promising has been thought to generate moral rules. Even in natural law and natural rights theories, promising has been seen as a way of creating conventional rights and obligations. A world without promises, it is generally assumed, would be a world in which persons simply could not reach agreements or rely upon one another.

We question many, although certainly not all, of these doctrines. We do not question the assumption that promises are, or are intended to be, assurances, or that they are usually interpreted to be assurances, for that is what the dictionary says they are, and our argument rests partly upon this premise. The persons we argue against, on this point, question this premise by attempting to redefine the meaning of "promise," holding that promises really do not assure that "one will do or not do" the promised thing.

We also do not deny that persons may sometimes, and perhaps even frequently, have obligations to keep their promises, or even that there may be a legitimate presumption in favor of promise keeping, for our main thesis is that *promise making* is wrong, not promise keeping. We do, however, reject the claim that the making of a promise *by itself* creates a moral obligation of any kind, actual or prima facie, or that it is the function of promises to create such obligations, whether by virtue of the meaning of the word "promise," by virtue of its illocutionary force, or by virtue of moral rules or social practices—all of which are positions that other philosophers have held. We deny these claims despite our agreement with many philosophers on the fundamental point that promises are assurances, or, more exactly, *because* they are.

A promise is an assurance that one will do or refrain from doing something. It says *nothing* about whether what is promised, or even the promise itself, is morally right or wrong. But even if it did, we contend, it would not eo ipso be obligation creating, for it does not follow from the fact that one proclaims to have an obligation that one therefore has one. Nor would promising create an obligation because some social rule or practice says it does, for such a rule or practice would be morally wrong. For the same reason, there cannot be a "natural" moral rule or principle which dictates that persons must keep their promises.

The moral rightness or wrongness of *keeping* a promise depends, not on the simple fact that a promise has been made, but upon the *content* of the promise, and hence upon whether or not keeping it (i.e., doing *that* thing) would be morally right or wrong, *all things considered*. One of the things to consider, of course, is the effect of keeping or not keeping a promise upon the person to whom the promise was made, but, obviously, others must be considered as well. Thus, our theory of promise keeping, presented at the end of the book, ties the duty to keep promises to the *reliance* that promises can and often do create. But much depends on whether what is relied upon is itself morally good and how such reliance weighs against other moral considerations.

On the question of keeping promises, many of our critics seem to hold a position similar to ours. They maintain that a promise ought to be kept only if there is no overriding moral obligation in conflict with keeping it. However, unlike us, they also assign a special moral obligation to promise keeping. They seem to believe that every promise, properly made, creates a duty of promise keeping, albeit a prima facie duty. By contrast, we argue that promises are not by themselves obligation-creating acts. The mere act of promising does not create any moral obligation—not even a prima facie obligation.

The mere making of a promise (the act of promising) does not and cannot by itself create any obligation, independently of the content of the promise and other moral considerations. This seems to be shown clearly by the consideration that a promise to do something morally wrong cannot create an obligation to do what is morally wrong. A promise to do something morally wrong cannot create even a prima facie obligation. This consideration shows that any obligation to keep a promise depends on the content of the promise. It also depends on a promisee's expectation or reliance, for, as most philosophers seem willing to allow, a promisee may release a promisor from a promise, thereby nullifying any obligation to keep it.

But if the making of a promise is an assurance, and possibly also a commitment to act in a certain way, then it is also a proclamation of intention to act in possible and perhaps even probable *opposition* to moral principles, rules, or institutions. If so, then the making of a promise is morally *wrong*. Indeed, promises are often made for just this reason, to assure another that one *will* rule out all other alternatives, including, if it so turns out, other morally required alternatives.

Now, the *keeping* of a promise may be morally permissible if it does not conflict with other overriding moral considerations, and it may even be required, but this consideration does not justify the *making* of promises. It does not justify promising because no one can, except in ignorance, sincerely assure another that a promised act will not conflict with duties to do other things. In fact, no one can know in advance, except with respect to the nonperformance of acts, that the keeping of a promise will even be possible, let alone that it will not conflict with other obligations. We argue, therefore, that promises are assurances of acts which cannot, with moral justification, be assured. They are, for this reason, immoral.

Put another way, promises cannot be used to reconstruct the moral world. Either promising changes future obligations or it does not. If it doesn't, then it doesn't create any obligations we would not otherwise have. If it does, it changes something that would have been obligatory or prohibited and makes it nonobligatory or permitted, or it takes an otherwise permitted act and makes it obligatory, rendering all otherwise permitted acts wrong. The latter alternative allows all duties to override promises, and the former allows promises to trump all duties and permissions.

CONDITIONAL PROMISES

The most commonly received response to our argument is to say something like the following: "Well, everyone knows that a promise is not a *guarantee* of future performance. Everyone knows that a promise might not be kept, and justifiably so. Nobody really expects people to keep their promises if other more important matters crop up, or if their promises are impossible to keep." If the objector is a philosopher, he or she might go on to say, "Promises create only prima facie obligations. They are conditional, not categorical, assurances, and if not explicitly so, then by virtue of background assumptions, or a mutual understanding between promisor and promisee about exceptions or acceptable excuses. Of course, keeping a promise can be morally right only if it does not conflict with other more important moral demands. Who ever thought it could?"[3]

At first glance, this argument appears to reduce our argument to absurdity, making it look like a real "howler," as some would say. But one should notice that this objection can be effective only if one backs off on the assumption that promises are assurances. Our opponents fail to notice that their position *weakens* the supposed obligation-creating power of promises. In their view, when persons promise to do something, they are not really saying they will do the promised thing but only that they will do so if certain unspecified conditions obtain. But such an assurance, we maintain, is not much of an assurance at all. People who ask for promises know what promising means: they know that they are asking for an assurance and not a "maybe-I-will-and-maybe-I-won't" response!

Of course there is such a thing as a conditional promise. If I promise you that I will play golf with you tomorrow unless it rains, we both know I'm off the hook if it rains. A conditional promise, explicitly stated, builds the conditions into the promise, but it is still a categorical assurance that one will do the act under those conditions. The same may be said of *implicit* conditions, of course, but the problem with implicit conditions is that they may not be known or agreed upon by both the promisor and promisee. Being implicit, they usually are not. Even philosophers cannot agree about whether there are any *general* conditions that qualify promises or about whether, if there are, *what* they are or *who* has the authority to determine them. Not much assurance can be given by a promise if the promisor and promisee do not know, or are not in agreement, about the conditions under which the promise is or is not supposed to create an obligation, or the conditions under which the promisee can feel assured that the promise will be kept.

Our contention, then, is that one cannot back off from the idea that promises are categorical assurances and still be talking about promises in the ordinary sense of the term. Conditional assurances certainly are assurances, but assurances with unspecified conditions are practically bound to be deceptive, especially when the promisor, or anyone else, can arbitrarily and unilaterally decide what the implicit conditions are or when they are satisfied.

Promising is paradigmatically, after all, a communicative act, and the strength of the assurance depends on what is being communicated by it. That, in turn, depends on what *both* the promisor and promisee understand by it. If they do not both have the same understanding, then they do not both understand what is being assured.

Philosophers have tried to meet this objection by placing upon promising the condition of a "meeting of the minds." But such a condition buries the problem we are addressing instead of offering a solution to it. The proposed solution ignores the fact that often there is no such meeting of minds and that, even if there were, such mutual understanding would not necessarily solve the problem. It would not solve the problem because neither the parties to a promise, nor anyone else, can make conditions morally acceptable by mere agreement. The conditions they agree upon, after all, may be immoral. So philosophers add another condition, namely, that promises, in order to be morally binding, must not be promises to do immoral things. But, in the first place, persons *can* promise to do immoral things, even if such promises are not morally binding. In the second place, even if a promised act appears to be morally acceptable at the time of making a promise, it may turn out to be morally unacceptable when it comes time to keep it. Thus, philosophers have added still another condition, putting upon promises a prima facie restriction, arguing, as above, that a promise might not hold if keeping it conflicts with (some or all) other moral obligations. But this, we argue, takes all of the punch out of promises, nullifying the assurance promises are supposed to give. The price of patching up the so-called practice of promising in order to meet the kinds of objections we raise is to render promises practically meaningless.

One should note at this point that our opponents are *changing* the ordinary meaning of the word "promise" by stipulation, not only weakening it, in one sense, but also by *strengthening* it in another. They weaken a promise by making it less of an assurance, but they strengthen it by holding that it is obligation-creating, as we and the Oxford Dictionary do not. Our position is that to give an assurance is *not* to create an obligation, even a prima facie obligation, as our opponents think it is. Just as we believe that neither society nor individuals have the power to make the keeping of promises obligatory, we do not believe that they have the power to determine, by simple declaration or agreement, what the conditions of justified promise keeping are, or under what conditions a person is excused from keeping a promise. The mere fact that the parties to a promise or members of society at large agree about when promises should or should not be kept (which they do not) would not by itself justify those conditions or exceptions. After all, people can agree on immoral conditions just as they can give and receive immoral promises. So it is not simply a question of what is accepted or agreed upon but a question of what is morally right. Acts don't become morally right by promising or by simply *saying* or agreeing they are. We take up this point later in discussing the so-called practice or institution of promising.

CONFLICTS OF DUTY

However, in much of our argument, and for the sake of argument, we *give* our opponents their position and ask them to consider what follows from it. That is, we try to reduce *their* positions to unacceptable consequences. Let us suppose that the conditions placed on promises are moral, and that they are generally known or even stated (say, in the form of social rules and practices), how would this resolve the problems we raise? Only so many positions are realistically possible. One may allow that *all* other duties or obligations override promises or that *none* do, or one may take some position in between. If none do, then persons have a moral obligation to keep their promises, no matter what. If all do, then a promise ought to be kept only if it does not conflict with *any* other duty. In the former case, the moral force of a promise certainly seems to be too strong, for it then nullifies the rest of morality, no matter what the promise is about. In the latter case, it seems too weak, for it is then practically no assurance at all. So, in principle at least, if not also in practice, one needs some way of determining the (other) duties a promise overrides and the ones it does not. No one, as far as we know, has even *attempted* to answer this question, but however the answer goes, we will show in chapter 4 that the proposed solution does not work.

One of the reasons it will not work is that the argument is still being made on *formalist* grounds, ignoring not only the *content* of promises but the *content* of other supposed duties or obligations as well. It matters, we argue, *what* is promised or, for that matter, *what* one lies about, or to whom and under what conditions, and how, after all, people are affected by such acts. Advocates of the prima facie duty view can never tell us just when a prima facie duty is an actual duty, and hence they can never tell us just when a promise ought or ought not be kept. Indeed, their own theory is a kind of unfulfilled promise. It consists of a number of *dodges* designed to avoid the conclusion that promises are immoral. The prima facie claim is more plausible when it comes to duties in general, for other duties are not, or at least need not be, assurances. They are guidelines for action and not commitments to act. They could not be guidelines and also commitments, for they would then, like promises, exclude other alternatives.

So we think that our opponents are guilty of some very fundamental confusions, and one of these is confusing the giving of an assurance with the creation of a moral obligation. Once one separates these ideas, one is able to see clearly that the one does not entail the other and may in fact oppose it. And this is not to say, of course, that a person cannot *feel* an obligation to keep a promise or that another person may not *hold* that person to his or her word. People do rely on promises, and because they do, a promisor may rightly feel an obligation to do the promised thing. But this consideration, all by itself, does not make promising or the keeping of promises right or obligatory.

It is possible to believe that persons ought always under all circumstances keep their promises, but such a code of conduct would be immoral. Such codes are not unusual. The code of the streets dictating that one should never rat on a friend, or the code of honor dictating that persons should fight duels when insulted, are codes, but they are not morally acceptable codes. The code of strict promising and strict promise keeping is such a code, for it can operate outside morality. The problem is that such codes cannot be reconciled with morality. Promising itself can be reconciled with morality only by weakening it, that is, by holding that promising does not override *any* obligations. However, this undermines the whole *point* of promising, namely, the giving of an assurance.

Consideration of the content of promises is important, for it seems unreasonable to hold that a trivial promise can override matters of great concern. The selection of examples intended to illustrate obligations of promise keeping can be affected by this consideration, for the duty to keep a promise, when such a duty exists, may depend on the seriousness or importance of performing or not performing the promised act. Our critique focuses on the question of whether there is a duty to perform an act simply because it was promised. This seems to us to be the focus of all the philosophic literature on promising, and we challenge our opponents to explain exactly what moral work promising is supposed to do. How does the mere act of promising, independent of other considerations, change the moral landscape? Promising either changes obligations in some determinable way or it does not. If it does, it *alters* our duties. If not, then it creates no obligations we would not otherwise have.[4]

Thus, to argue that promising is a prima facie duty that can be trumped by *all* other duties is to claim that promising leaves the moral landscape practically unchanged. On such an account, the keeping of a promise could rule out acts which would otherwise be permitted but not obligatory, but, even then, there is a serious question about whether promises should be kept in the face of other important but nonobligatory options. To argue, at the other extreme, that promising creates an actual obligation, or that promising overrides all other obligations, would be to hold that a promise wipes out everything on the moral map. The only other alternative is to take a position somewhere in between these extremes, but one would need to spell out which features of the moral map are altered by promises and which features are not. No one, as far as we know, has been able to point out what those features are, much less *why* some of them are changed by promises and others are not.

We have not tried to consider and refute every actual theory on promising, for we believe that every theory fits somewhere in our schema, but we do consider many actual positions as examples. Thus, we do not try to present a history of philosophical theories on promising or even a complete survey of recent literature. However, we are interested in showing that people do in fact hold the views we criticize, and hence that we are not arguing against "straw" persons. There are philosophers who have recognized the problem we point out and who have tried to solve it. We, in turn, try to show why their proposed solutions will not work.

RESIDUAL QUESTIONS

There are, of course, residual questions about our own theory of promising, and perhaps, even more fundamentally, our own theory of moral obligation. There may also be questions about how we think promising differs from other obviously related concepts like intending, predicting, agreeing, contracting, planning, and the like. Indeed, why or how do we think that the obligation to keep promises (when there is such an obligation) is different from other duties? Why do we not think that other duties involve promises?

With respect to related notions, such as agreeing and contracting, our position is that either these are assurances or they are not. To the extent that they are, or are intended or interpreted as such, they create the same problems. If they are not offered as assurances, the problem vanishes. If people take agreements or contracts to be assurances (i.e., promises) they may think that the mere fact of agreement or contract creates a moral obligation, and hence that it overrides other duties. If they do not so interpret them, the moral landscape, on their view, remains intact. But it is important to note that the very meaning of "agreement," for instance, is different from "promise." The dictionary defines "agreement" as "harmony of opinion, action, or character" and as "an arrangement as to a course of action." The giving of an assurance is not part of the definition. Take for example the statement, "I'm going to play golf tomorrow." It is not on the face of it an assurance, but another party, hearing this statement, may make plans accordingly, perhaps by planning to play golf also. But the speaker did not assure the hearer and certainly did not invite the hearer to play golf. But suppose they agree to play golf. The speaker agrees to play golf with the hearer at a certain time and the hearer also agrees that they will meet. Again, this is not explicitly a promise, although it may be taken to be such by the parties involved. It seems to us that everything depends on whether the speakers *intend* to assure, with the intent to create reliance. Even the intentional creation of reliance, however, is not necessarily the same as giving the kind of assurance offered by a promise, for a promise explicitly excludes other alternatives.

Evidence of this is that in making an agreement it is not pointless to ask for a promise in addition to the agreement. "I know you have agreed to be there, but do you *promise* to be there?" The person interrogated may then answer by saying, "I promise," *assuring* the questioner that he or she *will do* what they have agreed to do. But the person asked to promise might also say, "Well, I agree to be there, but I can't *promise*, because I might not be able to make it." The withholding of the promise does not nullify the agreement, but the giving of a promise does strengthen it, even cement it. This is what our opponents seem to miss. They do not seem to take promises seriously, even though they seem to believe, as we do not, that the act of promising creates a moral obligation. A promise to commit a murder does not create a moral obligation, but *it does assure that the act will be done, even though immoral.*

The same may be said of other obligations or duties. They are not, we believe, usually thought of as assurances, even if one ascribes to them, for we all know that they may be overridden by other considerations. A promise is different, for a promise makes the claim that an act *will* be done. It does not, on its face, allow either a moral or an immoral way out. A promise is violated if the promisor does not do the promised act, no matter what the reason. Again, it is not redundant to ask a person to promise to do his or her duty, but making a promise in such a case is still *wrong*. It is wrong because it rules out *not* doing one's duty when other overriding obligations conflict.

Either a promise adds something to a statement or claim or it does not. What it adds, fairly obviously, is an assurance, and the assurance is that the act *will be done*, even if subject to certain conditions. If it is not done under the conditions of the promise, then the promise is not kept, although, of course, one may be justified in not keeping a promise.

Our theory of obligation is simple enough. We hold that an act is obligatory when it is demanded by moral considerations or when moral considerations exclude all other alternatives. An act is prohibited when it is excluded by moral considerations, and an act is allowed or per-mitted when not so excluded. One of the purposes of moral reasoning is to try to determine which options are excluded and which are not.

Thus, on our account, a promise is offered precisely for the purpose of excluding all other alternatives, and this is what makes it wrong. It expresses the *intention* of excluding all other alternatives, but the inten-tion of doing so does not make it right, and it certainly does not make it obligatory. Promises are not obligation-creating acts. Both a promisor and promisee may *think* they are, but that does not make them so. Promising, we argue, cannot be used to rearrange or cancel out moral responsibilities. But it is precisely because people *rely* on promises, even to the extent of rearranging their lives accordingly, and have been led to do so by promises, that the making of promses can cause undue harm. Promises are misleading, and often viciously so, in a way that agree-ments or contracts, as we try to show, need not be, precisely because they allow for morally or legally acceptable alternatives.

We do claim at the end of the book that persons might have a prima facie duty to keep a promise because the reliance on a promise, created by the promise, may and often does tip the balance of obligations in favor of promise keeping. This is so even if, as we claim, promising is immoral (and even *because* it is immoral), just as one might incur a moral obliga-tion by immorally harming another. If one *immorally* creates an expecta-tion that is, all things considered, legitimate to satisfy, it then seems that one has an obligation to make good on that expectation, to prevent the harm that nonperformance would cause. But, again, this is not because promises all by themselves create moral obligations. They do not create any obligation if there is no reliance, or if, all things considered, keeping the promise is ruled out by other moral considerations.

Our position on the prima facie obligating force of some promises is different from those who claim flat out that a promise is prima facie binding. We hope that our readers will keep in mind this difference. We do claim that there may be an obligation to keep a promise, but we do not claim that promises all by themselves create moral obligations. If there is no reliance, there is no prima facie obligation to keep a promise. Also, unlike our opponents, we believe that keeping a promise may be overridden by prudential as well as moral obligations. We think that this is a strength; it means that a trivial promise may be overridden by a more serious prudential need. Our opponents who quickly assert that a promise itself has a prima facie moral standing have not thought through the implications of conflicts between prudential needs and moral obligations. If they claim that all prudential needs can create moral obligations, as utilitarians seem to believe, then to hold that promises create prima facie obligations is nearly ludicrous.

Finally, it is important to note that our opponents often use our own position against us, not fully understanding what our position is. They want to allow that the keeping of a promise may be overridden by other moral considerations, as we do, but they want to build such exceptions into the very *meaning* of promising, or into rules governing it. But this won't work because that is *not* what promising means, and, furthermore, there are no such rules except for rules proposed by philosophers, which not even they can agree upon. We take pains to show that the conditions which philosophers have placed on promising simply do not hold and that, in any case, there is no agreement among philosophers or ordinary people about what these conditions are. That is, there is no institution or practice or promising, in the sense of a "promising game," governed by rules determining when something is or is not a promise, or a justified promise, or a promise that ought to be kept. There are simply promises, and everybody, except philosophers, seems to know what they mean. They mean what they say, nothing more, nothing less.

People know that promises are assurances and, therefore, often rely on them. But people also know that there are unreliable promisors and hence do not always rely on what they say. They also know that something else might come up that prevents a promisor from keeping a promise. But they do not, for all that, usually misunderstand what promising *means*. They may in fact not take promises seriously because they know, or at least believe, that promises are often not kept. But, again, they still know what a promise *is*. What they apparently do not know, or usually do not realize, is that it is *wrong* to promise, for they have simply not thought it through. But we can't blame them for this, for most philosophers have not thought it through either.

Yet, sometimes, each and everyone of us is aware of the point that we are trying to make. We sometimes, perhaps often, say, "I can't really promise." "I can't promise *because* something else might come up." And when we say this, we are aware of the immorality of promising, even if we would not put it that way. To say one can't is not to say that one is unable but that it would be wrong to do so.

NOTES

1. *The American Heritage Dictionary*.

2. *Oxford English Dictionary*, Second Edition.

3. Jon K. Mills argues against us that a promise is justified if made and accepted in good faith and that such good faith involves an understanding that promises are conditional, not absolute commitments. This is an example of the argument that "everybody knows" that promises are not supposed to be kept if impossible to keep, or if keeping them conflicts with other duties. "The Morality of Promising Made in Good Faith," *Journal of Value Inquiry* 29 (1995): 575–76.

4. Holly Smith, in her article, "A Paradox of Promising," addresses part of the problem we discuss in her attempt to explain how persons can avoid abusively using "the moral power of promising to legitimize pernicious acts." But what she fails to consider, among other things, is that promises are assurances; hence, she fails to explain just why it is that, on her interpretation, promises are supposed to have the moral power she attributes to them. *Philosophical Review* 106 (1997): 165.

TWO

THE INCOHERENCE OF RECEIVED VIEWS

I shall further observe, that, since every new promise imposes a new obligation of morality on the person who promises, and since this new obligation arises from his will; it is one of the most mysterious and incomprehensible operations that can possibly be imagined, and may even be compared to transubstantiation *or* holy orders, *where a certain form of words, along with a certain intention, changes entirely the nature of an external object, and even of a human creature.*[1]

David Hume

Hume might have done well if he had both begun and ended his treatment of promises with the point he makes in the above quotation, explaining in between his reasons for thinking so. Instead, he tries to show that the force of promising, which, on his view, cannot be derived from nature, *can* be established by social convention—thus demonstrating that promises are really not so absurd after all! That Hume was wrong in thinking he could so resurrect promises from the graveyard of philosophic absurdities is a major part of the thesis we defend in the pages that follow. We try to explain why promising really is incoherent, and why, therefore, the accounts given by Hume and so many other philosophers do not make sense. Since, however, this thesis flies in the face of conventional views on the subject, and opposes received views in philosophy, we thought it would be wise to begin by surveying philosophic positions, indicating some of the things philosophers have said about promises, and including what many nonphilosophers appear to believe as well. But a number of these views run into difficulties, recognized by philosophers and nonphilosophers alike, that philosophers have tried to overcome by patching up their theories in one way or another, in a manner not unlike that of Hume. Few seem to have recognized that this patchwork only serves to disguise a fundamental flaw in the very idea of promising that is, we maintain, irreparable.

The mere fact that philosophic theories vary considerably in their accounts of the nature and binding force of promises indicates that promising is at best problematic and that the explanation of promises, although apparently obvious, is far from evident. It goes without saying that not all of the theories on promising can be correct, but, of course, not all theories are mistaken on every point, nor are the mistakes they make exactly the same. However, there is a tendency on the part of nearly all theories to attach undue importance to the need for promises in the first place. On this point, our position may appear extreme, but we argue that the world could do very well—and indeed would be better off—without them. Our claim is that promises do not satisfy the need for giving and receiving assurances, as many philosophers believe they do, and that, even if they did, they would not be the only way, or even the best way, of satisfying this need. More forcefully, and contrary to every received view we know, we maintain that, as a rule, the making of promises is an immoral thing to do.

Philosophers differ considerably on the question of the moral force of promises, or on the duty to keep them, both with respect to the question of when they are binding and with respect to the question of why they are when they are—or why they are not when they are not. But even here there is a general tendency to shift back and forth between the extremes of attaching too much or too little weight to the duty of promise keeping. The one extreme, not shunned by every philosopher, is to hold that the duty of promise keeping binds without exception. The other extreme is to hold, as act utilitarians do, that the duty to keep promises cannot override moral principles or any other moral duties, and hence carries with it little or no assurance at all. But others, believing that promises are assurances, find it necessary to weaken the assurances by allowing exceptions, or by placing conditions on promising designed to limit the kinds of acts promises can justifiably bind. Nearly all philosophers recognize, for example, that persons cannot be obligated to perform immoral acts, even if such acts are promised, so they claim that persons are not bound by immoral promises. But what they succeed in doing, we argue, is to take the assurance out of the promises, the very thing that promises are designed to do.

Promising involves many other problems, including, for example, differences in the beliefs of promisors and promisees about the binding force of promises, questions of a meeting of minds about what exactly is promised, and even questions about how long a promise may be said to hold or whether, in fact, a promise has been made. In philosophic discussions of these topics, it seems that promises are often confused with contracts, although these two things, similar in some respects, are not the same. Thus, promises are sometimes said to presuppose certain background conditions, such as a meeting of the minds, or, as Hume maintains, to depend on a social practice or institution that brings with it sanctions in cases of breach. Others, like John Rawls, argue that promises require practices stipulating game rules that determine when promises are valid or when exceptions are allowed. But such institutional backing, we claim, is not necessary and in fact does not exist. A practice or institution of promising, we hold, is not needed either for the making of promises or for the creation of a duty of promise keeping.

For all of this, we do not believe that persons are never obligated to keep their promises, for they often are—even if, and perhaps especially if, they should not have made them in the first place. People are, we maintain, responsible for the expectations and reliance they intentionally create. Thus we allow that, given reliance, there is a prima facie duty to keep promises, but we also hold that this duty may be defeated for many different reasons. We conclude that there is not much assurance to be had from promises and that what little assurance they provide comes not so much from any obligation creating force of promising as from the reliability of promisors. Reasonable reliance, we assert, is founded not on what we believe other people ought to do, morally speaking, but on what we believe they may be expected to do, based on induction from past experience.

In sum, that is our story. But let us begin with the received views and then show how our position is dictated by the problems they create.

RECEIVED VIEWS

Promises have been given considerable attention in the literature on ethics, even to the point of receiving an especially honored place. The duty to keep promises is regularly listed among the most fundamental of moral rules. Immanual Kant, for example, includes the duty to keep promises among his categorical imperatives, as justified by the principle of universalizability, and as one of the precepts of the moral law.[2] W. D. Ross rejects Kant's claim that moral rules are categorical imperatives, but he includes the duty of promise keeping in his list of basic, prima facie duties, and argues that it is self-evident, without need of proof.

> The general principles of duty . . . come to be self-evident to us just as mathematical axioms do. . . . In a precisely similar way, we see the prima facie rightness of an act which would be the fulfillment of a particular promise, and of another which would be the fulfillment of another promise, and . . . we apprehend prima facie rightness to belong to the nature of any fulfillment of promise.[3]

Social contractarians and rule utilitarians do not usually speak of the duty to keep promises as a fundamental moral rule or principle but, rather, as a derived duty, contingent on social institutions or practices. Rawls claims:

> That punishment and promising are practices is beyond question. In the case of promising this is shown by the fact that the form of words 'I promise' is a performative utterance which presupposes the stage setting of the practice and the properties defined by it.[4]

Nonetheless, on both accounts, the duty to keep promises has the power to override consequentialist considerations, as in the philosophies of Kant and Ross. John Rawls, for example, defending rule utilitarianism in "Two Concepts of Rules," argues that

> there are obvious utilitarian advantages in having a practice which denies to the promisor, as a defense, any general appeal to the utilitarian principle in accordance with which the practice may be justified. . . . It is a mistake to think that if the practice is justified on utilitarian grounds then the promisor must have complete liberty to use utilitarian arguments to decide whether or not to keep his promise.[5]

Indeed, in social contract theory, promising appears to play a double role, as a condition for the very creation of the contract and as a derived rule within the contract. When Hobbes, for instance, talks about renouncing and transferring natural rights, he immediately speaks of freely intending to take on an obligation, and of being bound, or of having a duty accordingly, holding, it appears, that it would be an *absurdity* for people not to do what they have contracted to do—despite his appeals to self-interest and his claim that there are no obligations prior to the contract.

> Right is laid aside, either by simply renouncing it; or by transferring it to another. . . . And when a man hath in either manner abandoned, or granted away his right; then is he said to be OBLIGED, or BOUND, not to hinder those, to whom such right is granted, or abandoned, from the benefit of it: and that he *ought*, and it is his DUTY, not to make void that voluntary act of his own: and that such hindrance is INJUSTICE. . . . So that *injury*, or *injustice*, in the controversies of the world, is somewhat like that, which in the disputations of scholars is called *absurdity*. For as it is there called an absurdity, to contradict what one maintained in the beginning: so in the world, it is called injustice, and injury, voluntarily to undo that, which from the beginning he had voluntarily done.[6]

Hobbes appears to clearly regard contracts as promises, for he points out that the keeping of a contract is the keeping of a promise.

> Again, one of the contractors, may deliver the thing contracted for on his part, and leave the other to perform his part at some determinate

time after, and in the mean time be trusted; and then the contract on
his part, is called PACT, or COVENANT: or both parts may contract
now, to perform hereafter; in which cases, he that is to perform in the
time to come, being trusted, his performance is called *keeping of
promise*, or faith, and the failing of performance, if it be voluntary, *violation of faith*.[7]

If, according to social contract theory, contracts are themselves
promises, or are founded on promises, then the duty to keep promises
cannot be derived from the contract but must already hold in a state of
nature. And if, as in Hobbes's theory, all other duties are dependent on
the duty of promise keeping, then the promise-keeping rule must function as *the* supreme moral principle. Indeed, it often seems to be so
interpreted in libertarian philosophies which hold that there are no
natural moral laws and that people can have duties only if they consent
to having them. But then, of course, there must be one duty that is not
dependent on consent, namely, the duty to do what one consents to do.

Promising has thus served as a model for self-created obligation—
a kind of almost magical way of creating duties by merely choosing to
have them. Indeed it seems only natural to hold, as John Searle has
maintained, that to promise is to "take on an obligation" to do what
one says, for that seems to be the whole point of promising. It seems to
be, in fact, what "promising" means. "I take it," Searle writes in "How
to Derive 'Ought' from 'Is'," "that promising is, by definition, an act of
placing oneself under an obligation."[8]

Few philosophers have questioned whether, as a rule, persons ought
to keep their promises. Nor have they usually doubted that promise
making and promise keeping are generally good and useful things to
do. Most assume that the making and keeping of promises—the "practice of promising," as many call it—is a building block of society,
needed for organized planning, cooperation, and the coordination of
actions. Pall S. Ardal remarks in his article "And That's a Promise" that
"the practice of promising is necessary in social life, in order that we
may take it in trust that people's future behavior will be of a certain
sort."[9] Referring to the practice of promsising, Stanley Cavell states that
"the very existence of human society and the coherence of one's own
conduct, depend upon it."[10] Even Henry Sidgwick, who otherwise has

serious reservations about promises, cannot help but remark upon their importance in society:

> The importance to mankind of being able to rely on each other's actions is so great, that in ordinary cases of absolutely definite engagements there is scarcely any advantage that can counterbalance the harm done by violating them.[11]

John Stuart Mill says:

> The important rank, among human evils and wrongs, of the disappointment of expectation, is shown in the fact that it constitutes the principal criminality of two such highly immoral acts as a breach of friendship and a breach of promise.[12]

Promising, or the duty to keep promises, has been accepted as a paradigm, and sometimes even as *the* paradigm, of morally obligatory behavior, and has thus been used as a *test* of moral theories. Even a skeptic like Hume, who raised serious doubts about promises, felt that he had to account for them within his theory. The question among philosophers regarding promises has been not *whether* there is a duty to keep promises, or even whether promising is an important social practice, but *how* to account for this duty. According to some, like Ross, there is no accounting for it at all, except to say that it is an underived rule that must simply be intuited.[13] But, for others, like Hume, it is justified on other grounds. Only avowed act utilitarians, such as J. J. C. Smart, have rejected the idea that persons are bound to follow moral rules of any kind, including promise keeping, and they have been roundly criticized by deontologists for this reason. Of the duty to keep promises, Smart writes:

> The rightness or wrongness of keeping a promise on a particular occasion depends only on the goodness or badness of the consequences of keeping or breaking the promise on that particular occasion. . . . If the goodness of the consequences of breaking the rule is *in toto* greater than the goodness of the consequences of keeping it, then we must break the rule.[14]

Contemporary rule utilitarians, apparently feeling the sting of criticism from deontologists such as Ross, have attempted to resurrect the duty to keep promises, indicating that the felt need to give a theoretical account of promising is very strong—even among consequentialists! Rawls, for example, specifically tries to meet Ross's criticism of utilitarainism in framing his own explanation of rule utilitarianism in "Two Concepts of Rules." He says:

> But certainly Ross is right in thinking that it strikes us as wrong for a person to defend breaking a promise by a general appeal to consequences. For a general utilitarian defense is not open to the promisor: it is not one of the defenses allowed by the practice of making promises.[15]

The emphasis on promises in theoretical ethics seems to reflect, of course, the importance placed on promises in ordinary life. Many people, if not most, appear to take promises seriously, holding others and themselves responsible for keeping them. Politicians are routinely thought to be scoundrels for failing to keep their campaign promises. Individuals often rely heavily on the promises of others, to keep secrets or appointments, to repay debts, or to discontinue bad habits. Failures to keep promises can result in serious loss, not only by frustrating expectations, but also by undermining other acts that are contingent upon the performance of promised acts. Because of harm caused by breach of contract, breaches of contract are subject to legal sanctions. As Thomas Scanlon observes in "Promises and Practices," people sometimes need to be assured, and promising satisfies this need.[16] And, since persons can be disappointed and even harmed by failures to keep promises, it seems important, even necessary, to hold promisors to their words. In a complex society, where people rely on one another for the performance of countless tasks, observance of the duty of promise keeping appears to bind the very fabric of social and moral life. Commenting on what he calls the promise and economic views of contract, Michael D. Bayles writes:

> The expected benefit of entering interactions involving commitments rests on the assurance that they will be fulfilled. The views' emphasis

on trust, beneficial reliance, and fulfillment of reasonable expectations all support legal assurance. Promises are more trustworthy if supported by law; beneficial reliance is more likely when the law enforces most commitments; and expectations and reliance are reasonable if the law will protect them.[17]

DEFEASIBLE ASSURANCES

However, this so-called practice of promising is not without its problems. Perhaps the most obvious difficulty with the rule that people ought to keep their promises is that it seems to have exceptions. The truth of the matter is that not all promises ought to be kept. It seems obvious that people should not keep promises to do immoral things. There are also times when, it appears, the keeping of, say, a relatively trivial promise should give way to a more important duty. That is why W. D. Ross dubbed the duty to keep promises, as fundamental as he thinks it is, a prima facie duty, to account for the possibility that this duty may conflict with other duties, and hence, in a particular case, not be an *actual* duty or obligation.

> I suggest 'prima facie duty' or `conditional duty' as a brief way of referring to the characteristic (quite different from that of being a duty proper) which an act has, in virtue of being of a certain kind (e.g., the keeping of a promise), of being an act which would be a duty proper if it were not at the same time of another kind which is morally significant.[18]

This consideration alone reveals that the mere fact of promising does not, all by itself, establish a moral obligation. That fact that someone promised, even truthfully, is not a sufficient reason for holding that person responsible for keeping the promise. However, this consideration alone does not tell us when, or under what conditions, promises are or are not binding. After all, people often disagree about when they should or should not be held responsible for keeping promises, so there appears to be a need for clarification on this point.

A number of philosophers have accepted this challenge, laying down conditions that, according to their analyses, must be met in order for a promise to be morally binding. According to these restrictions, only certain kinds of promises are supposed to be valid or genuine, and among these, only certain kinds are said to be morally justified. Many social contractarians have insisted, for example, that promises must be made freely or voluntarily, without coercion. Following Kant's dictum that "ought" implies "can," others, like von Wright, have held that persons cannot be held responsible for keeping promises that are impossible to keep, nor are they justified in making or keeping immoral promises.[19] Searle says:

> The conditions will include such things as that the speaker is in the presence of the hearer, Smith, they are both conscious, both speakers of English, speaking seriously. The speaker knows what he is doing, is not under the influence of drugs, not hypnotized or acting in a play, not telling a joke or reporting an event, and so forth.[20]

The list goes on, and, as one might expect, not all philosophers agree about each and every condition. The point, however, is that the determination of whether or not, on any particular occasion, anyone has an obligation to keep a promise now appears to be a rather complex issue—one that cannot be settled by simply appealing to the more general promising rule. Other factors must be taken into consideration, and one needs to know when a promise, or the duty to keep a promise, is or is not nullified by these considerations. Few theories, if any, seem refined enough to answer this question. Perhaps Thomas Aquinas was right in observing that principles can be known with certainty but that their precise application in particular cases is often doubtful, due to a variety of circumstances:

> The practical reason, on the other hand, is concerned with contingent matters, which is the domain of human actions; and, consequently, although there is necessity in the common principles, the more we descend toward the particular, the more frequently we encounter defects.[21]

There certainly seems to be plenty of room here for the act deontologist, or the emotivist or existentialist, to enter the fray, saying, "See, I told you so; you can't really make a determination by applying principles or rules—or by any process of reasoning at all!"

Although these points bear upon the theses we defend in the following chapters, there are, we believe, still other, more radical conclusions to be drawn. After all, if the problem posed by promising were simply a matter of getting clear about the rules of "the promising game," or about "the practice of promising," as it is sometimes called, one might actually succeed, after perhaps careful and diligent examination, in discovering what those rules are, or how they should be applied. If, indeed, promising were really a social practice or institution, a kind of game, so to speak, one might actually propose changes in the rules, in order to make them more consistent and complete, as the rules of games should be. In this respect, the promise-keeping duty appears to be no different from any other duty. The problem of knowing when promises should or should not be kept is, after all, no different from the problems associated with other moral rules that may conflict with one another and have exceptions. Every pluralistic system is faced with the difficulty of finding a decision procedure, and a moral theory that has more than one principle or rule is no exception.

Our contention is that there is something peculiar about promising—something especially problematic—that follows from the consideration that the promising rule can have exceptions, but also from a consideration of the nature and function of promises themselves. It is because promises are supposed to be *assurances*, we argue, that the consideration of exceptions to the rule of promise keeping becomes so troubling. According to our argument, the possibility, and, in many cases, the very real probability of justified moral exception undermines the assurance that promising is supposed to give. Thus, on our view, there are problems with promising that cannot be fixed simply by putting restrictions on it, or by adding more rules to the promising game. The so-called practice of promising cannot be fixed, we try to show, because it is incoherent.

THE CONCEPT OF PROMISING

At first glance, the concept of promising seems clear enough. People seem to have little difficulty using the expression, "I promise," or knowing what it means. Promising, or making a promise, means assuring someone that one will do, or refrain from doing, an act, or a certain kind of act, and saying, "I promise" is one way—perhaps the clearest way—of doing that. A parent promises his or her children to take them to the circus on Saturday. A wife promises her husband that she will stop smoking. Both promisors and promisees know that saying, "I promise to do X" is much stronger than saying, "I intend to do X," or "I plan to do X," or even "I shall try my best to do X." None of these latter expressions gives assurance that X will be done. Or, if they do, they are weaker assurances than a promise. A promise, one might say, is a very strong assurance, or an expression of intention to give a very strong assurance, but even this seems to fall short of what is meant. Saying, "I promise to do X," is much more like saying, "I *will* do X," *guaranteeing* that X will be done by me. It means, it seems, "I will do X, and you can count on that." "You can count on me; you can plan your life accordingly." That is why philosophers rightly talk about expectation or reliance. Promisees who take promises at face value, and hence at full value, take them to be assurances that the promised acts will happen, and hence that they can count on them. When a person fails to keep a promise, it is only natural to respond by saying, "But you promised; you said you would," or even, "You lied." Ardal underscores this point by arguing that promises "both state an intention of the speaker, and make an assertion about future action." He writes, "I both assert my intention to meet the promisee for lunch and also that I shall in fact meet him."[22]

The reader may be tempted to say at this point, "Wait a minute; your interpretation of the meaning of promising is too strong." The objection might be that no reasonable person thinks a promise is meant to *guarantee* performance, but only that the promised act will be done under certain anticipated or normal conditions. One might grant that promises are not usually stated in conditional form but hold, nonetheless, that there are certain background conditions that the parties involved assume (or should assume) must be met, in order for a promise to be binding. But this takes us back to the point made above: the recognition that the duty to keep promises can have exceptions, or that there are conditions under which promises may or may not hold. Thus, perhaps, anyone who understands the concept of promising should take this *caveat* for granted; namely, that the assurance provided by the duty of promise keeping is defeasible and may turn out to be not much of an assurance at all.

But is this part of the concept of promising? Perhaps the concept of promising is not so clear as it first appeared, for, if the assurance given by a promise is now understood to be *conditional*, a promise is not as much of an assurance as it first appeared to be. It now turns out to be more like, "I'll try very hard to do X, but if I fail, it will be because something prevented me, or something more important came up." So, if I promise you not to tell your very embarrassing secret to anyone, you can rest assured that I will not do so unless I think I have a good reason to break my promise. The trouble with this is that something cannot be a good reason for breaking a promise if *what is promised* is already thought to be conditional upon such reasons. That is, if the promise is conditional, and the condition is not satisfied, there is no obligation to break. In any case, a conditional promise, depending on the conditions, might not provide the requested assurance: in this case, the assurance that the secret will be kept.

This is not to say that persons may not take promises more or less seriously, just as they may attach more or less significance to telling the truth. But this has nothing to do with what is *meant* by promising or truth telling. Because we know that some people do not take promises seriously, in the sense that they regularly fail to keep them, or do not even care whether they do, we also know that we cannot rely on their promises, just as we cannot rely on hearing the truth from habitual liars. They know that by promising they are giving assurance and thus intentionally creating or trying to create expectation or reliance. That is, after all, how they may succeed in deceiving others. But they may, nonetheless, ignore or discount their promises. There are, in this sense, immoral promisors. For this reason, the mere fact that somebody promises is not itself sufficient reason for expectation or reliance: we also need to know that the promisor takes promises seriously. The strength of a promise depends on the reliability of the promisor. Even if we suppose that a promise creates an obligation, the obligation means little, by way of giving assurance, if the promisor cannot be counted on to do what he or she is obligated to do. Thus, although promising is a way of giving assurance, or of giving a guarantee, the assurance or guarantee depends as much on the habits of the promisor as on the promise itself. If a promisor is an habitual promise breaker, it would be good for promisees to know this, for they could then make sure to keep their options open, or simply not rely on the statements of assurance they receive.

That the mere saying of words is no guarantee of anything appears to be at least part of what Hume had in mind when he likened promising to the sacraments of the Church, pointing out that they seem magical at first glance, creating obligations by sheer fiat. Interpreting Hume, J. E. J. Altham writes:

> Hume correctly saw that even if there were such an act of mind as willing an obligation . . . , it would not follow that the performance of such an act would result in an obligation. . . . Hume indeed claimed that it was 'naturally unintelligible' that an act of willing an obligation should actually bring an obligation into being.[23]

But, in Hume's considered opinion, promises are really no such thing. Hume tried to show that promises and the expectation of promise keeping are based on *substantive* considerations, not a mere form of words: on the *reliance* of promisees and promisors' fear of censure. Indeed, his analysis of promises construed them to be more like contracts, according to which the *force* of agreements is backed by punishment for breach.[24]

There does seem to be something strange about promising, as Hume observed: something strange about the idea that persons can create obligations for themselves just by saying or declaring they have them. Indeed, promises have often been said to be performative utterances, very much like the sacraments of the Church, according to which the *saying* that one is doing something actually *constitutes* doing it. To say, "I do" in a marriage ceremony is tantamount to doing it, except for the consummatory part, and saying, "I swear" is to swear. Likewise, it has been pointed out that to say, "I promise," at least under appropriate conditions, is to promise. But what is it to promise? According to Searle and others, to promise is to "take on an obligation" to do what one has promised to do. Yet, fairly obviously, even if the meaning of promising is as strong as we have made it out to be, it does not follow from the mere fact that one *says* that one will do something, or even that one has an obligation to do something, that, therefore, one does indeed have the obligation. Some *link* needs to be established between the saying that one will do and the obligation to do: a major premise to the effect that persons must do, morally speaking, what they saythey will. In "The Promising Game," R. M. Hare writes:

> We cannot yet speak of placing upon ourselves an obligation just by saying, merely, "I place upon myself the obligation, etc." . . . "You have to adopt the constitutive rule or moral principle that one has an oblig- ation to do those things of which one has said `I (hereby) place upon myself an obligation to do them'."[25]

The question then, of course, is why should anyone accept this missing link, i.e., this premise or constitutive rule.

THE PROMISING GAME

The missing link, on some views, including those of Rawls and Searle, is the existence of a social practice or institution according to which the saying of the words, "I promise," or some equivalent, is *taken to be* a way of obligating oneself. It is the "done thing," as Stephen Toulmin would say.[26] Social institutions or practices are supposed to be analogous to games, according to which certain moves have certain meanings or implications according to the rules. In "the promising game," saying, "I promise" is a move which, according to the rules of society, constitutes taking on an obligation. The obligation created by promising, if not its very meaning, is "defined by the rules."[27]

There is, of course, a serious question about whether any such prac- tice or institution is really needed to explain how promises work.

Thomas Scanlon, himself a social contract theorist, disagrees with Rawls on this point, arguing that the duty to keep promises follows from a more general moral principle, and hence needs no special institution or practice to justify it.[28] P. S. Atiyah, analyzing the relationship between contracts and promises, claims that the existence or nonexistence of a practice or institution is an *empirical* question which, presumably, could fairly easily be settled.

> If and in so far as promising is an exercise governed by certain rules, an examination of the nature of those rules might be very illuminating. . . . But if there is one thing that is clear about the literature on promising it is the absence of any serious empirical content. The examples offered in the literature are usually trivial or whimsical and almost invariably hypothetical. They tell us nothing about the actual practice of promising as an existing social institution.[29]

Philosophers, however, treat the issue as if it could be settled by conceptual analysis. It seems that what is *meant* by an institution or practice may be settled by philosophical analysis, but the *existence* of any such thing does seem to be an empirical matter. If such a practice or institution did exist, it should not be difficult to find out what its rules are; after all, persons generally would need to know the rules in order to play the promising game. Even Rawls maintains that "it is essential to the notion of a practice that the rules are publically known and understood as definitive."[30] In point of fact, however, if there are any such rules, there is much confusion about them.

But, then, what is the moral force of practices or institutions? One would suppose that it is not the mere *existence* of a practice or institution that justifies actions within it but only the existence of a *justified* institution. But Searle claims that this sort of criticism is out of place. Speaking of the mistakes of philosophers on this point, he says:

> The first is a failure to distinguish external questions about the institution of promising from internal questions asked within the framework of the institution. The questions, "Why do we have such an institution as promising?," and, "Ought we to have such institutionalized forms of obligation as promising?," are external questions asked about and not within the institution of promising.[31]

What is or is not a correct move in the game of chess, for example, is a different question from the question of whether or not the game of chess is justified, or a good game to play. And there is some reason to believe that, in some cases, persons may be bound by existing practices, even if those practices are unjustified. They may be obligated to follow the rules of even bad institutions, or the bad rules of good institutions, until, say, those institutions or rules can be changed. But we do not suppose that philosophers think of the practice of promising as a bad institution, or that the rules in it are bad rules. What we find is that they have difficulty agreeing about whether there is any such institution at all, or, if there is, what its exact game rules are.

Let us suppose that there is a practice or institution of promising, justified according to more fundamental rules or principles, which does have rules in it that are also justified. Why should we do what that practice, or the rules of that practice, say we should? Well, one might answer, we have just assumed that the rules are good. Yes, but sometimes, as we have pointed out, even good rules can have exceptions. We are not automatically bound to do something just because a rule says we should—not even a very good rule. This takes us back again to the point of exceptions to rules in general, and, in particular, to the rule of promise keeping. The supposed institutional rule which says that saying, "I promise" is a way of taking on an obligation must be taken to mean taking on a prima facie obligation. In fact, it appears to be nothing more than the general promise keeping rule advocated by rule deontologists, only now with the added apparatus of a so-called social institution. But, as before, the force of promising is greatly weakened by this prima facie qualification, and the problem of keeping the assurance in the promise remains.

One might hold that a social practice or institution of promising can, and in fact does, exist, not only in the sense that a promising rule is justified by reason, or by intuition, as in the philosophies of Kant and Ross, but also in the sense that such a rule is accepted in a given society and is even acted upon or sanctioned by punishments or rewards. If it were a strict rule, holding that the obligation to keep promises is without exception, and if people regularly followed the rule, for whatever reasons, promises would indeed turn out to be strong assurances that could generally be relied upon. But, of course, such a practice would be immoral, for it would allow a person to discount entirely other moral obligations. A society might also adopt a weak promising rule that permits exceptions in many cases of conflict of duty, but such a rule would defeat the main purpose of promising, namely, giving assurance. Philosophers who claim that a social institution or practice of promising exists, or must exist, often wish to maintain that, in addition to the general promise-keeping rule, there is a list of other rules that determine when promises need not, and perhaps even must not, be kept. Such a set of rules could then provide assurance within a limited domain without ignoring completely other moral duties. However, we argue that there is no such list of subordinate rules that is generally accepted and that, even if there were, it could not be complete. There is no way of determining in advance precisely when the duty of promise keeping will override other duties and when it will not.

One problem with the game analogy, as several philosophers have noticed, is that there is a difference between rules that *define* acts, or moves within a game, and rules that *regulate* such acts or moves.[32] What it *means* to make a touchdown in football, for example, is quite a different matter from what players are allowed to do, or not do, in order to make one. The two notions are easily conflated in games, of course, because the desirability of making touchdowns follows from the object of the game; but the making of a touchdown is desirable only for the team that makes it, not for its opponent. Another difference, noted by philosophers of sport, is that games are artificial activities that are self-contained and cut off from ordinary life.[33] Thus, Searle's claim that, in a game, we can ignore external considerations is valid, up to a point, but not in real life, or in morality. We cannot in real life wholly separate the justification of acts by rules from the justification of the rules themselves. Certainly one might have argued, within the institution of slavery, that holding slaves is justified, or that slaves are simply property, but that does not justify the practice, and it does not justify acts within the practice. Even in a game like football, attempts to injure the quarterback are wrong, not simply because they violate the rules of the game, but also because it is immoral, generally speaking, to deliberately try to harm anyone.

In the received analyses of promising, there are two factors which are supposed to work in support of one another but which, upon examination, have not been reconciled. The one is the straightforward *meaning* of promising, the giving of an assurance, and the other, the moral *force* of promising, the creation of a moral obligation. The second appears to follow from the first, or to support it, for the obligation is supposed to hold promisors to their words, to make good on the assurance. And this might work well enough if there were no obligations other than those created by promises. But, even then, it is not always possible to keep promises and, under conditions where people make many promises, the keeping of one promise may still conflict with keeping another. The main difficulty is that no one can control future contingencies so as to assure future performance. There is also much more to morality than the keeping of promises, and other considerations are, sometimes at least, more important. J. E. J. Altham underscores several of these points, pointing out the possiblity that "some unforseen event takes place that makes it imperative to do something that would prevent the keeping of a promise" and that "the resulting conflict of obligations is a misfortune that one cannot be sure of avoiding." He argues, in effect, that one cannot use promises "to rejig the moral world."[34]

On our view, persons who have an understanding of the full range of moral responsibilities must realize that promises cannot be allowed, willy nilly, to interfere with or undermine the rest of moral life. But that is exactly what they must do if they are to make good on their assurances.

We are not arguing that persons are never obligated to keep their promises. Indeed, they sometimes are, because promises can create expectation or reliance. What we do maintain is that, as a rule, persons should not *make* promises: that the making of a promise, generally speaking, is an immoral thing to do. Once a promise has been made, however, even if immoral, there may be an obligation to keep it, for expectations may have been created which, morally speaking, ought to be met. Our focus on expectation, or reliance, calls attention to *substantive* considerations in promising, as Hume did in his analysis, but we do not appeal to any institution or practice of promising to support our position. Philosophers who appeal to the institution of promising, or the so-called promising game, appear to focus on *formal* considerations, or a *definition* of promising, to support their claims. They do seem to think, as Hume remarks in the quotation cited at the beginning of this chapter, that the duty to keep promises follows from the *meaning* of words alone, or from the uttering of them, because some social rule or practice says it does. The mere fact that a promise has been made is supposed to create an obligation, or at least a prima facie obligation, regardless of its content or the consequences of keeping it. But, as Hume observes, that is "one of the most mysterious and incomprehensible operations that can possibly be imagined."

We have no objection to calling promising a practice if what is meant by a practice is simply a kind of action frequently performed by members of society, referring, in the case of promising, to the fact that people often make promises, take them seriously, and rely on them. We merely wish to show that the practice of promising, understood in this sense, is unjustified, because it is either a deceptive offer of assurance or it conflicts with other moral obligations. But we allow that promises may create obligations nonetheless, by calling attention to the *content* of promises, or to the seriousness or triviality of what is promised, when considering how reliance bears upon obligation. We shall argue that obligations do not follow from promises alone, but from the fact that promises are relied upon, and only then if the importance of keeping a promise outweighs other moral considerations, or is demanded by them.

PROMISES AND CONTRACTS

Philosophers who speak of an institution of promising seem to think that promises are supported by the same sort of institutional apparatus as contracts are—something like the law. They not only compare promises with contracts but sometimes even conflate the two, thinking that promises and contracts are the same thing, or that promises are based on contracts, or contracts on promises. Thus, they suppose that the rules of promising are like the laws of contract, prescribing or defining what is or is not a valid or justified contract, and specifying legal actions that may be taken when contracts are breached. But, as we have noted, if there were such an institution of promising, we should be able to find it. The law is an institution, the government is an institution, schools are institutions, slavery was an institution in the United States, but where do we find the institution of promising? Assuming that conflicts will arise as to what a promise entails, we look to an institution to provide the basis or ground rules for determining how a promise should be interpreted. But there seems to be no such ground rules. This should lead us to suspect that there is no practice of promising, at least a practice that is well enough defined to save promises from the kinds of charges we make against them.

Promising is, of course, one of a whole family of concepts, including contracts, agreements, and commitments, according to which people express to one another, more or less forcefully, their intentions regarding future actions. Just how these concepts differ from or are similar to one another has been a matter of controversy, but it seems to be the case that, in ordinary language, their meanings sometimes overlap. Promises, contracts, agreements, commitments, and the like can all create expectation or reliance, and all can be used to enlist cooperation and coordinate future actions. But none of these, except promises, *assures* performance. Agreements or contracts, although statements that the parties involved will do certain things, perhaps in exchange for other things, are not, strictly speaking, assurances that acts will be done. Contracting to do something is, it seems, similar to promising, in that contracting to do something can entail responsibilities, but a contract is still not an explicit assurance. It is more like saying, "I will do it," and, "You can hold me liable if I don't," allowing for the real contingency that one may not do what he or she has contracted to do. People who enter contracts know that the parties involved may not perform, and hence that they may need to sue for damages, or simply write off whatever losses are incurred.

In cases of breach of contract, it is difficult to predict what the courts will demand by way of settlement, but they do not usually enforce contracts by making people do what they have contracted to do; instead, they hold them liable for nonperformance. The courts are there to adjudicate complaints when contracts are broken; they are not there to make sure that contracts are kept. Indeed, as contract law has evolved, more and more conditions have been placed on the making of contracts, and there has been less emphasis on the mere fact that a contract was made or an agreement reached. As we show in chapter 6, "Contracts and Promises," disputes tend to be settled more and more on the basis of legal principles, statutes, and precedents than according to the terms of the contract itself. This seems to indicate that the law has come to regard contracts not as promises that must be honored, but as agreements or plans that must, of necessity, be modified according to changing conditions.

Contract law, in effect, appears to have evolved out of and away from the promising model, according to which the statements or agreements of autonomous individuals are supposed to be honored, into a model for resolving conflicts according to principles and statutes. It has changed in a way, we are arguing, that our concept of promising itself should change, or be eliminated, in favor of a more serious consideration of moral principles and rules. Thus, the important consideration, in morality, as in law, is not whether we have done what we have promised or contracted to do, but whether what we are doing is right.

Nothing of moral value will be lost thereby. In the day to day business of life, little depends on promises and contracts in any case. One person places an order on the phone and another person fills it, without any explicit promise or contract being made. If part of the order is missing, the customer calls back and mentions it: the matter gets worked out between the parties involved. A contract or work order often has the benefit of spelling out in greater detail the terms of agreement, so there is a record of it, but contracts are rarely used for other purposes and are rarely taken to court. When they are taken to court, they are often settled in the same way a dispute would have been settled if there were no contract, except as the terms of the agreement are very often written down for the court to see. Even then, it is impossible to cover every detail of an agreement and illegal to enforce agreements that are harmful or unfair. Likewise, the fact that a promise was made, in lieu of or in addition to a contract, does not change the conditions of settlement, except as one or another party may have been led to act upon an agreement, or to have suffered loss—matters which may be actionable in any case.

Our point is that promises are not only deceptive and immoral; they are also unnecessary. Whatever legitimate work is done by promising can be done in other ways, without deception. There is little chance, of course, that people will stop making promises, or stop relying on them, because of the problems we cite. However, if we are correct, philosophers at least should give up the business of trying to make sense of promises, because, according to our analysis, there is no sense to make.

NOTES

1. David Hume, "Of Morals," in *A Treatise of Human Nature*, 2d. ed., ed. P. H. Nidditch (Oxford: The Clarendon Press, 1978), p. 226.

2. Immanual Kant, *Groundwork of the Metaphysic of Morals*, sect. 2.

3. W. D. Ross, *The Right and the Good* (Oxford: Clarendon Press, 1930), p. 32.

4. John Rawls, "Two Concepts of Rules," *Philosophical Review* 64 (1955): 30.

5. Ibid., p. 16.

6. Thomas Hobbes, *Leviathan*, pt. 1, chap. 14, para. 7.

7. Ibid, para. 11.

8. John Searle, "How to Derive 'Ought' from 'Is'," *The Philosophical Review* 18 (1964): 83–87.

9. Pall S. Ardal, "And That's a Promise," *Philosophical Quarterly* 18 (1968): 236.

10. Stanly Cavell, *The Claim of Reason* (Oxford: The Clarendon Press, 1979), p. 298.

11. Henry Sidgwick, *The Methods of Ethics*, 7th ed. (London, 1907), p. 442.

12. J. S. Mill, *Utilitarianism* (1861; reprint, Indianapolis: Hackett Publishing Company, 1979), 59.

13. Ross, *The Right and the Good*, p. 19.

14. J. J. C. Smart, "Extreme and Restricted Utilitaraianism," *The Philosophical Quarterly* 6 (1956): 345.

15. Rawls, "Two Concepts of Rules," p. 15.

16. Thomas Scanlon, "Promises and Practices," *Philosophy and Public Affairs* 19 (1990): 207–208.

17. Michael D. Bayles, "Legally Enforceable Commitments," *Law and Philosophy* 4 (1985): 325.

18. Ross, *The Right and the Good*, p. 19.

19. Georg Henrik von Wright, "On Promises," in *Practical Reason: Philosophical Papers*, vol. 1 (Ithaca, N.Y.: Cornell University Press), pp. 83ff.

20. Searle, "How to Derive 'Ought' from 'Is'," p. 4.

21. Thomas Aquinas, *Summa Theologica*, in *Phiosophy in the Middle Ages*, ed. A. Hyman and S. Walsh (Indianapolis: Hacket, 1973).

22. Pall Ardal, "And That's a Promise," p. 226.

23. J. E. J. Altham, "Wicked Promises," in *Exercises in Analysis*, ed. Ian Hacking (Cambridge: Cambridge University Press, 1985), p. 12.

24. "When a man says *he promises anything*, he in effect expresses a *resolution* of performing it; and along with that, by making use of this *form of words*, subjects himself to the penalty of never being trusted again in case of failure." David Hume, "Of Morals," p. 224.

25. R. M. Hare, "The Promising Game," *Revue Internationale de Philosophie* 18 (1964): 407.

26. Stephen Toulmin, *The Place of Reason in Ethics* (1950; reprint, Chicago: The University of Chicago Press, 1986).

27. Rawls, "Two Concepts of Rules," pp. 3–32.

28. Scanlon, "Promises and Practices," p. 201.

29. P. S. Atiyah, "Promises and the Law of Contract," *Mind* 88 (1979): 415–16.

30. Rawls, "Two Concepts of Rules," p. 24.

31. Searle, "How to Derive 'Ought' from 'Is'," p. 3.

32. See, e.g., B. J. Diggs, "Rules and Utilitarianism," *Philosophical Quarterly* 1 (1964): 33–44.

33. See J. Huizinga, *Homo Ludens* (London: Routledge and Kegan Paul, 1950) and B. Suits, "What is a Game?" *Philosophy of Science* 34 (1967): 148–56.

34. Altham, "Wicked Promises," p. 8.

three

PUTTING PRESSURE
ON PROMISES[1]

A prince never lacks legitimate reasons to break his promise.
                                        Niccolo Machiavelli

Howadever many differences one may find in the doctrines of moral philosophers, there is at least one point on which most seem to agree: that there is typically some sort of duty or obligation to keep promises. Yet philosophers differ considerably in their explanations of why there is such an obligation, or about the conditions under which it may be said to hold. Some, for example, maintain that the duty to keep promises is derived directly from some moral principle or rule, which is not itself dependent on social practices, and others argue that the duty to keep promises is dependent on a social practice, albeit a very important and even necessary practice. Some, in turn, interpret the duty to keep promises in a strict sense, allowing that few if any other considerations may override this duty, and others interpret it in a weaker sense, allowing that this duty is only prima facie.

Thus, among philosophers there seems to be significant ambiguity about the moral force of promising. It is just this ambiguity which tends to vitiate the claim that there is any clear principle or practice which governs promise keeping. The fact of the matter is that people interpret obligations stemming from promises in widely different ways, and philosophers do not seem to be of much help in resolving these differences. This absence suggests that, as a matter of practice, the moral force attached to promises is highly subjective, even capricious. Not only may a promisor and promisee have different intentions and expectations at the time a promise is made, but either may change his or her intentions or expectations over time. As a consequence, whether so intended or not, promises often turn out to be misleading and deceptive. A promisor, for example, may intend his or her promise to be binding in a weak or prima facie sense, understanding that many other considerations may override the obligation to keep it, while the promisee may interpret the promise in a strong sense, and hence place undue reliance on its being kept. The supposed duty to keep promises often trades upon such ambiguity in harmful ways. In the following sections we examine various types of ambiguity and conflict involved in acts of promising which seem to nullify the duty to keep promises or undermine the very assurances that promises are supposed to give. Our analysis begins by identifying several philosophical views on the nature of the obligation to keep promises in order to show that philosophers themselves do not agree about when promises are binding or why they are. We then point out that there is a number of reasons, generally recognized by moral theorists, for considering certain types of promises to be degenerate, in the sense that it would be morally wrong to make such promises, or in the sense that it would be morally wrong to keep them. We then extend the question of degeneracy to cover more controversial cases, labeled by us as cases of near degeneracy, and then to apparently normal cases as well. Our aim is to show that many of the problems that arise in what seem to be clearly degenerate cases also arise in the class of cases called nearly degenerate and in seemingly normal cases as well. In doing so, we intend to place pressure on the idea that promises can create moral obligations, not only in clearly degenerate cases of promising, but also in nearly degenerate and normal cases. Indeed, we raise the issue of whether there is or even could be any case of promising which escapes degeneracy, in the sense that promising creates a special obligation to keep the promise and hence makes good on its moral assurance.

PHILOSOPHIC VIEWS ON PROMISING

Promises are typically linguistic acts which are thought to create moral obligations. There is always a promisor and a promisee, even though, in unusual cases, these may be the same person. While the promisor creates the obligation by saying, "I promise" or by making some similar statement, the promisee, by virtue of the obligation, is supposed to have the right to make a moral claim against the promisor. But what sort of claim, and under what conditions? Well, to do the thing promised, one might suppose. But what if the promisor cannot do what is promised or realizes that it would be a morally wrong thing to do? Suppose the promisee releases the promisor from the promise, or turns out not to rely on it? The variety of opinions held by philosophers on these and related issues begins to suggest that the answers are far from being obvious or clear.

There are at least four distinguishable views on the nature and binding power of promises. The view which interprets the obligation to keep promises in the weakest sense is probably act utilitarianism. Act utilitarianism places great emphasis on objectively determinable moral obligations. Since it has only one principle which is supposed to determine what is right or wrong in all cases, it holds that no one can ever be obligated to do anything other than what the utilitarian principle itself dictates. Thus, there appears to be no reason to attach any special weight to promises or promise keeping. One ought to keep a promise if and only if keeping the promise produces the greatest utility.

Promises can affect utility, for they can create expectations, and the satisfaction or disappointment of expectations is an important utilitarian consideration. But, according to act utilitarianism, nobody has an obligation to keep a promise just because he or she has promised. Keeping a promise does not always maximize utility. Thus, the theory has been criticized for failing to recognize the moral force of promises, or for undermining the very assurances promises are supposed to give. As the criticism goes, no one could ever count on a utilitarian's doing what he or she promises to do. Yet act utilitarians seem to understand more clearly than other philosophers that promising cannot create obligations that conflict with moral principles. They realize that keeping a promise is morally justified when it accords with higher moral principles and that it is not justified when it does not.

The second and more rigorous view about promising is that it is a conventional practice, much needed in human society. It would be unfair, a moral violation of reciprocity, not to abide by our promises; thus, according to this type of theory, promises do establish a special moral obligation. The moral obligation that follows from a promise may come from sympathy,[2] or the contractual binding power of fair social conventions,[3] or simply from well established social practices, including linguistic practices.[4] Once a promise is made, a new obligation exists, and one that is uniquely established by the act of promising. This is not the case with the utilitarian for whom promising per se does not establish any unique obligation.

The conventional or practice view, in distinction to utilitarianism, is a relatively strong view because it maintains that a promise creates a new and unique obligation. However, since this type of theory recognizes that duties to keep promises may conflict with duties or obligations of other kinds, it also tends to qualify or restrict the binding power of promises. It is mainly this consideration which leads to differences of opinion about exactly when promises are or are not binding.

The third view appears to be even stronger because promising is thought to be governed by a moral principle[5] or a moral rule,[6] and hence can create a moral obligation even if no social practice exists. Although promises are made by individuals, and the use of the word "promise" may involve a linguistic rule, the moral force or authority of promises is not thought to be dependent upon or relative to an individual's personal morality or to social conventions. All people are bound by their promises just as they are bound not to lie. Nevertheless, it may be that the principle or rule is quite complex. For example, on some accounts, the principle or rule is said to be binding only if the promisor is sincere, or if the promisee relies on the promise. Such a theory may also hold that only certain types of actions are proper objects of promises, e.g., threats or immoral promises are not really promises or at least do not create moral obligations. Again, since there may be more than one moral principle or rule, the duties to keep promises must, sometimes at least, give way to other moral considerations.

The fourth view, the honor view, provides the strongest version of the obligation created by promises. It holds that promises are, or are similar to, pledges or vows that reflect the integrity of a person's moral character. Under this, the honor view, there appears to be no practice and no objective moral rule or principle which governs promises. The moral force of promises is derived from autonomous agents who bind themselves by their promises. According to such accounts, a person may make a promise to himself or herself, or a promise may be binding even after the promisee releases the promisor from the promise—or even after the promisee dies![7] Since, apparently, according to this type of theory, there are no objectively determinable obligations, there is no possibility of conflict between promises and objective duties. However, it still appears that promises can conflict with other subjectively determined duties, such as other promises.

These four views on promises are presented simplistically in order to map out some of the broader areas of disagreement. In assessing such disagreement, it is important to keep the point of promising in mind: it is intended to establish assurance that the promisor will do what is promised. To the extent that disagreement over the nature of promising is endemic, promises fail to provide this assurance. The problems stemming from the existence of such a variety of basic views is compounded because there are important theoretical disagreements within each group; furthermore, some of the views mentioned are qualified by stipulating that certain types of promises are degenerate and hence not binding at all. This latter qualification adds to the confusion about promising, because a degenerate promise on one view may be acceptable under another. Indeed, the disagreement about which promises are or are not degenerate (in the sense of not being considered genuine promises in the first place, or in being counted as genuine promises but not morally binding) shades off into the question of the conditions under which promises generally either ought to be made or ought to be kept. In reviewing various types of apparently degenerate cases, and then some apparently less controversial and even paradigm cases of promising, as we shall do below, we will show that the very considerations which render the seemingly degenerate cases morally objectionable also tend to vitiate the seemingly normal cases as well.

DEGENERATE CASES

The reasons for breaking promises, we submit, are also reasons for regarding promises as degenerate in the first place. The only difference seems to be that, in the case of supposedly degenerate promises, the objection to keeping them is foreseen or should be foreseen by reasonable people, whereas, in other supposedly normal cases, it is not.

Consider the following type of degenerate promise:

> Promising the impossible: A promises x to B, and x is considered by A, and perhaps by B, to be impossible to perform, e.g., cure an incurable disease, be in two places at once, lend money a person does not have, etc.

This is probably the most obvious type of degeneracy; as such, a promise to do the impossible may be discounted immediately, just because (if ought implies can) nobody can be obligated to do the impossible. Of course, the impossibility may be knowable but not known or considered by either party at the time the promise is made, or it may become apparent later. In the meantime, the promisee may rely on the promise. Promises to do the impossible are made, perhaps frequently so. For example, an impossible promise might be made to save a person in some seriously dangerous situation. Because the person in danger relies on the promise, he or she might not attempt other possible routes of defense or escape. Thus, the promise may turn out to be not only foolish but harmful.

Although most philosophers would probably agree that promises to do the impossible are not morally binding, or should not be made, academic discussions of such issues are almost beside the point. If people rely on them, they are vicious, and if people do not, there is no expectation to disappoint.

Other types of degenerate cases easily come to mind:

> Promising the immoral: A promises x to B, and x is considered by A, and perhaps by B, to be immoral e.g., rob a bank, go against one's parent's wishes, torture someone, get revenge, gang up on another, etc.

Here, it seems, the whole point of the promise is to provide a moral reason for doing an immoral act. But, since a person cannot be obligated by a promise to do something immoral, making or eliciting such promises appears to be wrong. Such promises, typically, are not morally binding. This conclusion clearly follows from any theory which holds that there are objectively determinable obligations or duties which can override the duty to keep promises, but the fourth view, mentioned above, may run into difficulties in this type of case. If the integrity view does not recognize objective duties which can conflict with promises, it cannot discount the binding power of promises on those grounds. It may even wish to maintain that there is, after all, honor among thieves. But, even then, it would seem, it must recognize the possibility that some promises may be inconsistent with other promises, or with other subjectively determined duties or obligations.

Promising the immoral suggests that a promise will or should be reconsidered whenever an opposing moral obligation intervenes. But different people have different ideas about their own moral obligations. Many people have a sense of balance among obligations: for many, a more serious obligation overrides a less serious promise. Evaluations of the seriousness of promises are bound to occur. Some will regard a seemingly insignificant promise, say to lend a pencil to a friend, as terribly important, perhaps because it was promised. Others might view a seemingly serious promise, say to take a friend to the airport, as a nearly insignificant matter, perhaps because the friend has available alternative means of transportation. Of course, many aspects of moral life involve similar ambiguities. These ambiguities are especially noteworthy in promising precisely because, as we have mentioned, promises are intended to provide assurances.

Threats appear to be much like promising the immoral. In a threat, A promises x to B but B does not want x, some harmful event. Since a threat is a promise to do harm to another, carrying out a threat would be morally wrong, all things being equal. It would also seem strange, for the same reason, to say that the promisee has a right to make a claim against the promisor, to receive harm, and it is highly unlikely that a promisee would want to make such a claim. This is not to say that threats are never justified, however. For example, a parent may, with good reason, threaten a child with punishment. To enforce discipline, a parent may rightly feel that, generally speaking, such promises ought to be kept. But few would hold that, even then, the promise ought to be kept just because it was promised. Sometimes at least, leniency would be in order. In other words, the parent would be free, morally speaking, to break his or her promise. The mere fact that such a promise had been made would not nullify other moral considerations—in this case, the welfare of the child. Yet, philosophical considerations aside, people do make such promises and promisees are in fact threatened by them. It is just because they are taken seriously that they can perform the function of threats.

> Promising the unlikely: A promises x to B while A knows that the occurrence of x is highly unlikely.

Promising the highly unlikely is degenerate because a promise cannot assure a highly unlikely outcome. As obvious as this is, it underscores a further problem with promising. Sometimes a person who knowingly promises the unlikely is simply yielding to social pressure. If pressure is put on A to make a promise, A may accede, knowing that the promise will not be kept. Promises are often made in such coercive or semicoercive situations. Pressure is brought to bear on persons to make promises (when they believe it would be better not to do so) based on close personal or business relationships. Persons may also promise the unlikely in order to influence promisees. For example, an auto salesperson may promise an unlikely quick delivery of a car to pressure a buyer to sign the contract. A promisee is (unfortunately) likely to respond to a promise in a way that is different from a mere statement of intention. So another side of promising the unlikely is the possible exploitation of the promisee. Thus, in many cases, promises mask coercion.

> Promising the ridiculous: A promises x to B, and x is considered by A, and perhaps by B, to be foolish or ridiculous, e.g., promising to stand on one's head if B wins the game, promising to walk to Kansas if Cleveland wins the pennant, etc.

Many ridiculous promises are also quite improbable. The categories of degeneracy are not mutually exclusive. Promising the ridiculous, in a pure case, involves, for example, the inane but perhaps easily doable. Typically, all the parties to the promise understand that the promise was not serious. It is a degenerate promise because it appears that no obligation is established. There are cases, however, in which one or the other party believes that the promise was not meant in jest. The promisee may then hold the promisor to performing the act in question. Such circumstances often lead to disappointment, even hostility. Doing the thing promised may not mean doing something immoral, or even something difficult, but it may mean placing undue importance or priority on something which, all things considered, should not be given that much time or attention. Promising the ridiculous is not a trivial category precisely because what is ridiculous to one person may be serious to another. This suggests that promising may require a "meeting of minds," as does a contract. But if so, almost all promises, as they are conventionally made, fail to be binding.[8]

NEAR DEGENERACY

It would seem that any reasonable view of promising would reject the kinds of degenerate cases mentioned above. And if the list of degenerate promises were clear, ambiguity over promises would be reduced. But the trouble is that there is controversy among philosophers and ordinary people over which types of case are clearly degenerate. Moreover, there are still other less obviously degenerate types of case that also raise difficult questions, and there is likely to be even less agreement about these. There is, for example, some similarity between promising the improbable and promising the distasteful.

> Promising the distasteful: A promises x to B yet A does not want x because x is not to A's benefit; A has no other obligation to do x, but is pressed into doing it by B's insistence, or because A feels obliged to do x for B, e.g., promising a friend to go on a date with a person thought to be thoroughly obnoxious.

Some people find it difficult to resist those who request promises, and this involves, perhaps, a kind of moral or personal weakness. If promises create special obligations, then personal weakness may place people under obligations to violate their own interests. It would seem better for people not to make such promises. A person could say, instead, "I'll try to do this for you," "I hope to be able to do it," or "I'll give that careful consideration." But when such promises are expected, even demanded, people are pressured to compromise their own interests or tastes.

> Promising the superfluous: A promises x to B, yet, under ordinary circumstances, A would do x without promising to do it, e.g., A borrows $5.00 from B, on the understanding that A will return it during the next pay period, but B insists that A promise to return the money after being paid.

Promises are superfluous when the actions in question would be performed without the promise, or when other accepted obligations or other forms of social assurance provide the desired security. Superfluous promises may seem harmless, but they also make it seem as though promising does some important work. They create the appearance that the outcome is assured. But superfluous promises may provide an illusory assurance. Such assurance is illusory when a change in circumstances, perhaps even a small change, provides a good reason for breaking the promise. Problems involving changes in circumstances lead to a wide ranging category of near degeneracy: the recalcitrant future.

> The recalcitrant future: A person promises an action that seems unobjectionable but, because of the future course of events, the promised act becomes impossible, distasteful, improbable, or immoral.

No matter how unobjectional or normal they appear, all promises are made in the face of a future which cannot be fully predicted. Thus, all promises, even promises taken to be paradigmatically normal, lie close to near degeneracy. A promise may seem unobjectionable at the time it is made, but, because of unforeseen circumstances, keeping the promise may turn out to be impossible or morally wrong.

Promises are made in the face of a future which is, to one degree or other, uncertain. Every reasonable person realizes that some future change of events may nullify a promise. How, then, can promises provide assurance? Given uncertainty, promises seem to create illusory assurances and may, therefore, disappoint expectations. Since such uncertainty affects even the most ordinary of promises, it would seem that firm statements of intention, or even mere statements of intention, are preferable to acts of promising.

Part of the recalcitrance of the future has to do with the simple passage of time, which necessarily involves a change of circumstances. How long do promises hold? What connection does a prior self have to a subsequent self who may be obliged to keep the promise? As people age, their views often change; to what degree does a previous promise bind a person who has developed significantly different views? A similar question can be asked about physical change: as people grow older their capacities change. The passage of time creates new possibilities and new limitations which can affect obligations to keep promises. Promising, it seems, is an attempt to bind actions in the future which cannot be bound.

Finally, the requirement of special assurance exposes the asymmetrical nature of promises. Significant promises typically occur in circumstances where mere statements of intention are thought to be inadequate. Giving assurance often means that there is a disproportionate gain for one or another of the parties involved, such that exploitation or coercion, even if mild in nature, may be present. Promises are asymmetrical because they are thought to establish an obligation on the part of the promisor and a right on the part of the promisee. Such asymmetry itself seems to require moral justification, because, on the face of it, it appears unfair. Several of the cases mentioned above illustrate this unfairness. There may be not only an undue burden on the promisor, but, as we have illustrated, undue burden on the promisee, and hence unjustified dependence on the promise itself.

THREE CASES

The following examples are meant to show that seemingly normal or beneficial promises suffer from problems similar to cases of degeneracy or near degeneracy.

> Case #1. Professor Smith hates college meetings. She will not attend next Thursday's meeting unless Professor Harris also attends. Although Harris says she is going, Smith wants to be sure. Because of Smith's insistence, Harris eventually promises to go.

This appears to be a perfectly normal promise, perhaps even a paradigmatic case of promising. The promise cements Smith's resolve to go, and she plans her life accordingly. Let us suppose that Harris goes to the meeting with Smith, perhaps only because Harris feels obligated to keep her promise. This seems to be a noncontroversial case standing in support of the worth and efficacy of promising.

To begin with, however, we should note the asymmetrical nature of the promise. The promise is supposed to assure Smith that Harris will attend the meeting, presumably even if Harris later finds it inconvenient or simply does not wish to attend, but Smith does not thereby give any such assurance to Harris. She could, of course, but if she does not, she is free of moral obligation in a way that Harris is not. The promise puts a moral burden on Harris but not on Smith.

Secondly, on the face of it, the promise appears categorical. It is the seemingly categorical nature of promises which provides the appearance of assurance: in this case, that Harris will attend the meeting, no matter what. But is such assurance genuine? Can it be? Smith and Harris should both recognize future contingencies that could render the promise null and void. Therefore, it seems, they should both recognize that the promise is really not categorical but conditional. If so, the assurance supposedly provided by the promise begins to look less assuring.

Harris herself may take either a strong or a weak view of promising. If she has a strong view, Smith may, with good reason, rely on her promise. But suppose something quite important comes up: Harris's father becomes ill and needs her help at the time of the meeting.

Should she go to the meeting at the cost of her own family concerns and obligations? A strong view of promising, in this case, would be quite harmful. According to a strong view, attending the meeting would be the morally correct action, even though the promise, concerning a relatively trivial matter, conflicts with a rather serious moral obligation.

Let us suppose that Harris takes a weak view. She believes that if circumstances change in any significant and unexpected way, she may be justified in breaking her promise. Suppose also that she is completing an article for a publication deadline. She decides to turn her attention to the paper and miss the meeting. She believes that Smith, a fellow academic, will surely understand her difficulties. But it turns out that Smith does not understand (after all Harris *did* promise) and insists that Harris keep her promise. Harris views this as exploitative and fails to show up for the meeting. The point is that the ambiguous nature of promising undermines the intended assurance, rendering it illusory.

The next example is a bit extreme, but it represents an ingredient in all promises: the fact that people often change beliefs, commitments, attitudes, or habits, over time. Even if it were clear whether a promise is initially intended in a strong or weak sense, such contingencies would remain. Given these contingencies, the following questions arise: How long does a promise hold? What sorts of changes in the promisor or in the promisee make a promise invalid? What sorts of changes in beliefs about promises invalidate them? When considering the following example, the reader should keep in mind that even fairly subtle changes in personal attitude can greatly affect the value of a promise.

> Case #2: Kevin, at age twenty-seven, promised his uncle, a priest, that he would say the rosary every day. Now Kevin, fifty years old, no longer believes in prayer. But Kevin is a philosopher who believes in a deep self and in the creation of moral obligations through promises. He says the rosary each day, but expects to stop when his uncle, now ninety-seven years old, dies.

If promises are self-created, they seem to depend on a "stable" self standing behind the promise. If we take a Cartesian view of the self—as a deep self[9]—a promise is binding for life. Kevin faces this problem. It would seem strange to hold Kevin to his promise, even if he continued to believe in prayer. But since Kevin stopped believing, it appears ridiculous to hold that he is still obligated to pray.[10]

If the self is a deep self, a strong interpretation of the duty to keep promises would commit persons to performing actions in the future that are foolish. But if the self is like Derek Parfit's self,[11] promises could easily become void. In our example, the fifty-year-old Kevin could be viewed as a different person from the Kevin who made the promise. The problem is that the efficacy of promises is contingent on a lack of significant change in the promisor's identity, for such a change can nullify the duty to keep the promise.

Our final example reveals the personal nature of obligations established by promising. It may seem that sometimes, perhaps often, a promise reinforces or even establishes morally correct behavior. It may even be the case that the most important function of a promise is to support morally correct behavior. This seems to be the case with Alice's son.

> Case #3: Alice's son is under-aged but often drinks and drives while intoxicated. He also believes that promises create strict moral obligations. However, he does not think that drunk driving is morally wrong. By withholding use of the car, Alice persuades him to promise that he will never drink when he drives the family car. Alice is convinced that he will keep his promise, but, in fact, he does not. Undaunted, Alice then succeeds in persuading her son to promise that he will never drive and drink, in anyone's car under any circumstances.

Promises like this appear to produce a kind of temporary, even if unstable, gain. It is an ironic fact that many people take promises more seriously than other more objective obligations. Playing on this, Alice appears to improve the situation. But her son continues to misbehave because of his attitude about drunk driving. Notice here that the mother pressured him to promise by refusing the car. Promises, we have said, often do involve coercion. Instability arises from the coercion. Alice's son, like many other promisors, may, with some justification, begin to view his promise as invalid. He may reason that he has no moral obligation because the promise was coerced. Although he takes a strong view of promising, he does not feel bound by a promise he did not freely make.

Suppose Alice and her son have a fight. They no longer talk to each other. Alice's son therefore views any promise he made to his mother as void. He reasons that he made the promise to his loving mother but that his mother is a different person now. Since the intended promisee no longer exists, the promise is not binding. Eventually his aging mother dies. Then he is even more convinced that he is released from his promise. Thus he continues to drive while intoxicated.

The odd thing about Alice's son is that he has a conscience about keeping promises but not about other more important moral responsibilities. This is often the case among people who believe that promises create strict moral obligations, for they must then believe that promises override other moral considerations. If Alice's son had more respect for other moral considerations, it would not have been necessary to elicit a promise from him in the first place—a promise which, it turns out, he could nonetheless discount. Thus, although he thought valid promises were morally binding, he had no difficulty in finding reasons for thinking that his promises were invalid.

CONCLUSION

The three examples above show how promises that appear normal, and hence seem to avoid degeneracy, can easily lapse into degeneracy or near degeneracy. This suggests that there may be something fundamentally wrong with the very idea of promising: the idea that a promise can serve the purpose of giving assurance by creating a self-imposed obligation. If we are correct, the assurances supposedly provided by promises are either illusory or immoral, for such assurances could be genuine only if other more objective duties were ignored. Even then, there are other contingencies and ambiguities which undermine the assurances that promises are supposed to provide.

For these reasons, promising seems to be a morally unjustified practice. It is tainted by a notion of personal honor that is entirely too subjective and too ambiguous to provide any genuine social advantage. By relying on promises and keeping promises, people are often exploited. At the very least, they are often disappointed. The answer, it seems, is not to instill a stronger sense of promising, or of personal honor, but to rely more on objective obligations: principles of justice and nonmaleficence, for example, and upon truth telling, contracts, or explicit agreements, where the parties involved know that they cannot reasonably assure performance but understand that they may be held liable if they fail.

NOTES

1. Joseph P. DeMarco and Richard M. Fox, "Putting Pressure on Promises," *The Southern Journal of Philosophy* 30 (1992).

2. For example, David Hume, *A Treatise of Human Nature*, 2d. ed., ed. P. H. Nidditch (Oxford: The Clarendon Press, 1978), pp. 552, 525.

3. See John Rawls, *A Theory of Justice* (Cambridge, Mass.: Harvard University Press, 1971), pp. 344–50.

4. See John R. Searle, *Speech Acts* (Cambridge: Cambridge University Press, 1970), pp. 54–63.

5. See Thomas Scanlon, "Promises and Practices," *Philosophy and Public Affairs* 19 (1990): 205.

6. See Bernard Gert, *Morality: A New Justification of the Moral Rules* (New York: Oxford University Press, 1988), pp. 128–29.

7. For example, R. S. Downie, "Three Accounts of Promising," *The Philosophical Quarterly* 35 (1985): 267–71; Michael H. Robins, *Promising, Intending, and Moral Autonomy* (London: Cambridge University Press, 1984), pp. 85–87.

8. Almost all of the distinctions and issues raised in this paper would have to be taken into account to establish a clear meeting of the minds. The issues to be taken into account range from the strength of the obligation to the sorts of personal changes that could invalidate a promise.

9. Derek Parfit thinks of the self as a continuous stream of thoughts, hopes, and recollections. He distinguishes his view from the self as a Cartesian substance, or a deep self. *Reasons and Persons* (Oxford: Clarendon Press, 1984).

10. This example works if we take "saying the rosary" as merely performing the appropriate actions and saying the appropriate words. If we think of it as an action with special meaning, then Kevin is no longer capable of performing the appropriate actions.

11. Parfit, *Reasons and Persons*.

four

THE IMMORALITY OF PROMISING[1]

Good resolutions are useless attempts to interfere with scientific laws. Their origin is pure vanity. Their result is absolutely nil. . . . They are simply cheques that men draw on a bank where they have no account.

Oscar Wilde

The purpose of making a promise is to assure someone that the promised act will be done. People think that this assurance creates valid expectations because it is backed by a moral duty self-imposed by the promisor. Without such assurance, a promise may be deceptive. But a genuine assurance, backed by a special moral obligation, is morally problematic. Can people justifiably obligate themselves, in advance, to keeping their promises, in the face of other possible moral obligations? We argue that they cannot. Promising is, as a rule, immoral: stated bluntly, it is either an advance declaration of intention to do the immoral under knowable or unknowable contingencies, or else it is a deceptive, and thereby immoral, offer of assurance.

Most of the philosophic literature on promises focuses on the supposed duty or obligation to keep promises rather than upon the morality of making promises. Various authors have maintained that, under certain conditions, promises may be broken, and perhaps even ought to be broken, when, for example, keeping a promise is immoral. But they have not argued that promising itself is morally wrong. Indeed, they have maintained that the practice of promising is an important social institution: a practice that is not only morally permitted but also, in some sense, necessary.[2]

Our thesis is radical in this respect. We intend to attack the position that promise making is, generally speaking, a morally acceptable thing to do, and also, a fortiori, the stronger position that promising is a morally necessary social institution. However, we hold our position precisely because promising is generally supposed to create a special obligation to do what is promised, for whatever reason such an obligation may be said to hold.[3] We shall argue, in short, that it is generally wrong for people to commit themselves to doing, or not doing, a particular sort of thing in the future just because, by so doing, they commit themselves to disregarding, or discounting, other moral considerations.

We assume that by promising, or by simple fiat, persons cannot nullify moral principles, rules, or obligations that are otherwise binding upon them. However, the making of a promise expresses a person's intent to so disregard or discount such principles, rules, or obligations; or else, a promise fails to provide genuine assurance. Promises are made to assure someone that one will do the thing promised and hence that one will in fact so disregard or discount at least some other moral considerations. For this reason, the making of a promise is, generally speaking, an immoral thing to do. It is a commitment to do something even if doing that thing turns out to be morally wrong.

Here is the dilemma. Either the supposed duty to keep promises overrides other considerations or it does not. If it does, it renders those other considerations null and void. If not, a promise cannot serve its function: it cannot, with *moral* weight, be used to give assurance.

This argument holds whether one interprets promising in a very strong sense, as committing a person to do what is promised, and hence as taking on, or intending to take on, a moral obligation to do the promised thing, or if one takes a weaker view on promising. One might attempt to avoid the dilemma by claiming that promising creates a prima facie obligation; this is tantamount to saying that a person who makes a promise will keep it, or intends to keep it, if he or she is moral, if keeping it does not conflict with any other more serious moral duties. But that, in turn, is tantamount to saying that the promisor *might not* keep the promise, weakening its assurance.

In their various analyses of promising, philosophers tend to shift from one horn of the dilemma to the other, or they try to slip between the horns by compromising, attempting to have it both ways at once. Most agree that promising creates a special moral obligation but then, upon reflection, recognize that the obligation cannot hold in all cases. They put conditions on promising supposed to save the special obligation while at the same time respecting other moral considerations. When it comes to conditions for making promises, the sincerity of the promisor,[4] the acceptance of the promise by the promisee,[5] and the supposed morality of the promise itself[6] have been mentioned. Conditions have also been placed on the obligation to keep promises; a promisor is said to be released from the obligation if the promisee agrees to this release,[7] or, by some accounts, if compensation is made,[8] or, finally, if fulfilling the promise conflicts with other duties or obligations.

But we cannot have it both ways at once. A promise is a promise. It is not merely a prediction or a statement of intention, nor is it simply a contract or an agreement.[9] In stating the conditions under which promises are supposed to hold, or under which a person is obligated to keep them, promises are often confused with these other types of act.[10] Promising is different from these other types of act because promising is supposed to create a special moral obligation. In addition to the expectation or reliance dependent on a prediction, a statement of intention, an agreement, or a contract, words like "I promise" add an *assurance* that the promised act will be done. Reasonable people understand that predictions, intentions, contracts, and agreements, all allow a moral way out, even if they impose a penalty for nonperformance. But insofar as a promise assures, it must exclude other alternatives even when these alternatives involve moral obligations, and precisely this special feature of promising makes it immoral. Putting conditions on promising chips away at the assurance; excluding them places promising in conflict with other obligations.

If a promise can be negated by too many other unspecified duties or obligations, it loses its force as a promise. However, it may appear that, if promises are limited by a list of special circumstances under which they may be defeated, involving other moral obligations or practical considerations, the value of a promise, as creating a strong moral obligation, may be maintained. Promises would then be thought to bind only within a limited domain. But if this limited domain remains large, promises would still be subject to our original objection. This is so because a large domain means that only a few other moral obligations can override the promise. Thus, the promisor commits himself or herself, in advance, to violating those other moral obligations which do not override the promise. Within this large domain the potential conflict with other moral obligations makes immoral the act of creating a special obligation. If the domain is small, then promises fail as assurances. Of course, even if the domain is small, other moral obligations may be overridden by the promised act. While there may be fewer such violations, promising is still immoral. It is immoral because, by an act of will, simply by making a promise, regardless of the content of the promise, one gives oneself the right to violate otherwise proper moral demands. Only if all moral obligations override the promise can it avoid the charge; but then the immorality involved in promising involves deception.

An example will illustrate these points. Suppose Ms. Smith borrows $50 from Mr. Jones. By borrowing, she owes Jones $50 and has incurred an obligation, albeit a prima facie obligation, to repay Jones $50. Suppose Smith says she will repay at 12 noon tomorrow. Suppose they sign an agreement, and Smith is known to be an honest person. We can predict that she will keep her agreement. She has a sincere intention to repay. But Jones is not satisfied. He is worried that his money will not be returned on time. So he asks Smith to promise she will repay on time. What more does the promise add?

By promising, Smith may be supposed to have incurred a new, added moral obligation in addition to and more binding than the agreement to repay her debt. But, if we interpret her promise as binding in a weak prima facie sense, it appears to add nothing to her duty to repay. Any conflicting duty that would override her agreement would also seem to override her promise. If, on the other hand, we interpret her promise as binding in a strong sense, genuinely assuring payment, force would be added to the agreement, but at the expense of requiring her to ignore other possibly conflicting duties. The promise would state her intention to so act. Thus, promising appears to do something that, morally speaking, it cannot do. It creates the illusion of adding moral weight to an agreement by binding the promisor to commit a potentially immoral act. The only way a person could be bound by a promise is if, in keeping with other moral obligations, the promised act is morally permitted. But no one can know, at the time a promise is made, that the promised act will be justified. In fact, calls for promises are usually made in response to concerns about nonperformance; otherwise the promise would not be needed. Promisors can commit themselves to keeping promises only by intending to override some potential conflicts of duty. If they are unwilling to ignore the possibility of such conflict, they cannot in good conscience offer assurance.

A SCHEMATIC VIEW

Philosophic views on the nature of promises range widely, between the one extreme of holding that promises are categorically binding, and hence override all other moral considerations, and the other extreme of holding that the duty to keep promises is overridden by any and all conflicting moral principles or rules. Neither of these extremes is very attractive, and so probably receives little support. The first preserves the strong assurance that promises appear to give, but at the expense of subordinating, indeed even canceling, all other moral requirements. Shunning this extreme, philosophers have regularly allowed that promises to commit (at least some) morally wrong acts cannot be morally obligatory. They would reach the second extreme if they maintained that promises cannot justifiably be used to override any other duties or obligations, but this extreme gives little or no weight to promises and subverts the function of giving assurance.

Thus, philosophers have generally taken the position that promises may be overridden by some, but not all, other moral considerations. Under any view between the extremes, a promise is supposed to create a new obligation, sui generis, differing from other obligations, and hence in possible conflict with any one or more of them. The question of the strength of a promise, then, or the strength of its assurance, may be represented by determining what other types of duty or obligation it overrides and what other types of duty or obligation override it.

In this section we present a schematic representation of the weight of moral obligations. This is meant to illustrate our objection to promising. We are not suggesting that such a representation can accurately account for moral obligations generally because we hold that the determination of moral obligations is a more complex issue. We merely want to use this representation to indicate that, no matter what force one takes a promise to have, one's position falls victim to the above dilemma.

Suppose we live under a web of moral obligations consisting in, among others, the obligation to do no harm, to be just or not to be unfair, not to tell lies, and to keep agreements.[11] Each obligation (O) is labeled with a unique subscript from the natural numbers, for example O_3. The set of obligations, including compound obligations, such as the obligation not to harm by not telling a lie, are represented,

$$\{O_1, O_2, \ldots, O_n\}.$$

Within this set can be placed an obligation O_p to keep promises. A promise may be made about any O_i, or about any other action not part of the set of moral obligations. Thus, person A can promise to B that A will keep an agreement, not tell a lie, or walk the dog.

We may suppose, then, that a promise creates obligation O_p in addition to the set of other ordinarily binding obligations, with the function of assuring, morally speaking, that an action will be performed under O_p. To be a genuine morally binding assurance, O_p must be made with the intention of overriding at least some other moral obligations, depending on one's view of the strength of a promise.

If obligations are listed in order of their binding power[12] such that obligations higher in the list (that is, with a greater subscript) are binding except under the most extraordinary moral circumstances and obligations lower in the list may be overridden more easily, a view on promising can be represented by placing Op lower or higher in the list:

(1) $<O_1, O_2, O_p, O_3, \ldots, O_{n-2}, O_{n-1}, O_n>$.

(2) $<O_1, O_2, O_3, \ldots, O_{n-2}, O_p, O_{n-1}, O_n>$.

(1) represents a weaker position on the moral strength of a promise than (2), a more rigorous view of promising.

The above-mentioned ordering may seem overly simplistic. The relative weights of obligations, one may suppose, is not determined simply by kinds of acts but also by the relative seriousness of the acts involved. That is, serious lies should be given more wight than trivial lies, and the same may be said of obligations of other kinds, including the obligation to keep promises. Thus, instead of adopting a pure rule-deontological view of morality, one might adopt a mixed view, according to which, say, consequentialist factors are taken into account. On such an account, the position of a promise on the list would be affected by the amount of expectation or reliance it created, or by the consequences of satisfying or disappointing such expectation or reliance, and the same consideration would hold for other obligations as well.

Accordingly, one may think that the problem can be solved by refusing to give promising a fixed spot on the list. Instead, promising could be thought of as a floating obligation. Indeed, all of our moral obligations may float in relation to one another. If a particular harm is serious, avoiding that harm would be higher on the list. Promises may then be placed higher or lower on the list depending on the seriousness of doing the promised deed. If one makes a promise about a serious matter, or if the promisee needs greater assurance, the promise would occupy a higher place on the list. But the question then is whether the fact of promising does anything to place the obligation higher on the list. If it does nothing, then the promise is superfluous. If, however, the promise makes a difference, making a serious matter even more serious, then the original dilemma must still be faced. Another very serious obligation, one that might have been an actual duty but for the promise, is now overridden by the promised act. The promise restructures the moral order.

In a recent article, "On Promising without Moral Risk," Daniel Kading appeals to an order of obligations in order to avoid the risk of moral conflict created by promising. His effort is noteworthy, for our purposes, because he recognizes that promises cannot be genuine assurances if they stand in constant danger of being defeated by other obligations. "Promising sincerely or in good faith," he emphasizes, "involves the intention of keeping one's promise."[13] But this intention cannot be sincere if the promisor knows that other obligations may override the promise. This is the problem, concisely stated:

> How could a conscientious person, at the time of making a promise, decide to keep it if he believed that he might, as events developed, find himself faced with an overriding obligation?[14]

The answer he proposes is that a conscientious person could avoid moral risk by qualifying, "at the time of promising, his promise in such a way as to make it impossible for an overriding obligation to arise."[15] By "moral risk" he means the possibility that a promise, considered morally obligatory, will be overridden by some higher obligation. By promising a person can create a moral conflict in which one or another moral responsibility must give way. But Kading believes that such moral risk can be avoided, and hence, in effect, that our problem can be solved. Basically, his answer is that promises always bind, but they do so because promises are always conditional.

Kading points out that, since at the time of promising the future cannot be predicted with complete accuracy, conflicts between duties of promise keeping and other duties may be expected or unexpected. With respect to unexpected events, on Kading's view, promises are already qualified, even without specification, by existing customs and practices. He claims that obligations can be arranged, as in our schema of moral duties, in a "certain order of importance" according to community standards and that this order is normally understood by both promisors and promisees. When another obligation overrides a promise, both promisors and promisees understand that the promise becomes "inapplicable." Failure to keep a promise in such a case, he says, "would not (ordinarily) be construed as a decision to break the promise: consequently there would not (ordinarily) be any promise-claim to weigh against other considerations."[16] Thus, in ordinary circumstances, persons may be expected to know when a promise holds and when it does not. There is, ordinarily, no deception, for a promise is understood to be conditional.

With respect to expected events, however, Kading maintains that promises can be specifically qualified, and hence continue to be binding, even in the face of conflicting obligations:

> For example, if I promise to repay a loan at a certain time believing that my family will probably suffer greatly if I keep the promise, it is understood nonetheless that I am promising to repay it under those circumstances. . . . It is understood also that no unexpected developments could make the promise inapplicable unless they involve consequences of a *higher order* than the expected suffering of my family.[17]

This is an example of what we mean by the immorality of promising; in this case, presumably, the promisor could avoid the suffering of his or her family if only the promise were not made. But once it is made, then, on Kading's view, the suffering becomes morally acceptable. Apparently, in the case of expected events, a promisor can rearrange the existing order of moral obligations by specifying, at the time of promising, which other obligations the promise will override. Without such specification, he says, a conscientious moral person could not sincerely intend to keep a promise.

Thus, Kading attempts to show how moral conflict can be avoided by building into a promise, at the time of promising, the conditions under which the duty to keep it will or will not hold. Moral risk can be avoided in expected circumstances by specifying other duties the promise will override and, in unexpected circumstances, by assuming exceptions determined by community standards. Promises are thereby supposed to retain their full obligation-creating force, for a promisor could, given such specified and unspecified conditions, sincerely intend to keep the promise.

Of course, as we point out in the next chapter, there is an important difference between sincerely intending to keep a promise (which is something a person might do under almost any circumstances) and actually having a duty to keep it, for a person might sincerely intend to do something that is morally wrong. The primary difficulty with Kading's analysis, in the case of expected circumstances, is that he allows the promisor's stated intention to override the existing moral order. Promisors, he seems to think, can simply rearrange duties by fiat, making otherwise wrong acts right. This is hardly an acceptable solution to the problem of moral conflict.

Kading's other idea that, in the case of unexpected events, promises are conditioned by an existing order of obligations also runs into difficulties. In the first place, there seems to be no such order, or, if there is, it is not generally known, and even if known, we could not simply assume its acceptance. Undoubtedly, people do sometimes agree about when a promise will or will not hold, but in the case of unexpected circumstances especially, it seems highly unrealistic to suppose that we can know in advance when promises will or will not be overridden by other considerations. One problem with trying to solve the problem of moral conflict by building exceptions into the rules is that no one can ever know fully, in advance, what the exceptions will be. This is a special problem in the case of promising because promises are supposed to be assurances. Promises can indeed be conditional assurances, but conditions cannot be used to qualify the assurance, at the time of promising, unless they are known. Furthermore, Kading's position becomes less plausible if one takes into account the idea that promises, by their very nature, are supposed to *alter* the order of existing obligations. They alter it by either creating an entirely new obligation, which must be placed somewhere on the list, or by giving added weight to an otherwise existing obligation, changing its position on the list.

Neither of Kading's moves solves the problem of conflict because neither takes the problem seriously. Allowing for the possibility of conflict at the time of promising, or telling it to go away, does not make it disappear.

As Kading recognizes, a person would not be sincere in promising if he or she did not fully intend to keep the promise. But that is exactly why we have held that promising is immoral. Kading himself seems to admit as much, for he cautions:

> One can and should, before promising, weigh the merits of expected events which, if they occurred, would give rise to a conflicting obligation: and (ordinarily) one ought not to promise if it is believed that the occurrence of any of these events would give rise to an overriding obligation.[18]

But why should a person be so cautious about promising if he or she could simply eliminate conflict by specification? Indeed, why any specification at all, for Kading also says that "unless specifically qualified to the contrary, a promise is always applicable under expected circumstances."[19] This is the exact opposite of saying that promises are inapplicable in the face of conflicting obligations (unless specified to the contrary) and, if true, would eliminate all need for caution about possible conflicts. In unexpected circumstances, community values, understood by members of the moral community, are supposed to determine the sense of the promise. But if community standards hold in the case of unexpected events, why not in the case of expected events as well? Furthermore, if promisors can state that promises bind in expected circumstances, then why not also in unexpected circumstances?

Kading recognizes the problem we address in this chapter, but he does not solve it, and does not solve it because it is unsolvable. If he allows promises to be trumped by other moral obligations, then a promise is not a genuine assurance. But if he allows promises to override other obligations, he permits the subversion of the moral order. Promises cannot both be genuine assurances, and hence override other obligations, and also be subject to nullification by other obligations. Persons cannot be subject to an objective moral order (whether determined by reason or by society) and also be free to change that order by promising. There can be no promising without the moral risk.

PROMISES AS PRIMA FACIE BINDING

Much of our argument in this chapter has been aimed at the positions of philosophers who believe that the dilemma we set forth can be avoided by claiming that promises create prima facie obligations. So interpreted, it is thought that promises need not override other moral values, for, in cases of conflict, they would give way to more serious obligations. On this view, if there is no conflict, the obligation created by a promise becomes an actual obligation. But part of the problem is that, to our knowledge, nobody has been able to explain adequately how promises weigh against other moral considerations.

To say that duties of promise keeping are prima facie appears to mean that such duties sometimes trump other duties and sometimes not. But we need to be able to specify when they do and when they don't. Such specification needs to be made in order for promisors and promisees to know when duties of promise keeping hold, or how the assurance given by a promise is morally conditioned, or, indeed, how much assurance a promise is supposed to give. Thus, to challenge our opponents, we have presented an artificial schema intended to show how the power of promises can be represented relative to other moral demands. We have invited the reader to think about which sorts of obligations really can or cannot be overridden by an obligation of promise keeping.

We believe, of course, that there is really no way of making up such a list, and hence no way of making good on the claim that promises create prima facie obligations. Even if there were, it would not follow that such conditions are generally understood and accepted, as they would need to be if promisors and promisees are to have a meeting of the minds about what exactly is being assured. Vagueness, or arbitrariness, erodes the assurance.

Our schema runs into difficulties, we noted, because it seems to ignore the relative seriousness or importance of keeping a promise relative to the seriousness or importance of conforming to other moral requirements. Much seems to depend on the *content* of a promise and not on the simple fact that a promise is made. This consideration weighs against the claim that promises—mere acts of promising—create prima facie obligations. It is generally supposed to be the very act of promising that creates a prima facie obligation and not the content of the promise or the importance of doing the promised thing. If a prima facie duty of promise keeping did arise from the content or importance of keeping a promise then, obviously it would not arise from the act of promising alone. And the case of immoral promising, we have pointed out, clearly illustrates that the act of promising alone cannot create a moral obligation—not even a prima facie obligation— because there can be no prima facie obligation to do the immoral.

In order to label a case as an instance of promising the immoral, it would be necessary to consider, even before making a promise, whether keeping it would conflict with other duties, and it would also be necessary to know in advance that certain other duties override promises. This consideration seems to support the view that promises can be overridden by other duties and also the view that we can know which other duties override promises. But what it does not show is that promising has an independent moral force that weighs against other duties. Promising the immoral does not supply a reason for doing the immoral which then gets defeated by the promise's immoral content. A promise to do the immoral is not a morally acceptable reason at all. A promise to commit murder is not a reason in favor of committing murder which then, upon analysis, gets defeated because it is opposed by a rule against killing. Promising to commit murder is not a reason for murdering that weighs against the harm of committing murder. But this is just what the act of promising would have to be if promises alone created prima facie obligations.

When W. D. Ross coined the phrase "prima facie duty," he repeatedly used the example of promise keeping to illustrate his point.[20] He maintained that moral rules, discovered by intuition, are hypothetical imperatives and not categorical imperatives. He pointed out that moral rules can have exceptions, especially when there is a conflict of rules. On his view, apparently, moral rules, which express prima facie duties, are sufficient for determining that actions are right or wrong in particular cases (actual duties) unless they conflict with other overriding rules or other prima facie duties. A prima facie duty may be said to be a duty "all things being equal" and an actual duty a duty "all things considered." Unfortunately, Ross did not explain clearly how persons are supposed to determine when one rule overrides another, or specifically, in the case of promise keeping, how one is supposed to know when the duty of promise keeping overrides other duties. It seems that there would need to be some principle for ordering the rules, or persons would need to appeal once more to intuition to settle the issue.

It seems worth noting that, in talking about prima facie duties, Ross was talking about moral rules as *reasons* for or against acts. A rule provides a prima facie case, as it were, for or against acting in a particular way. An act of promising creates a prima facie obligation because there is a moral rule that says we ought to keep our promises. The rule functions as a reason, in competition with other reasons, for performing the promised act. But, if so, the very act of promising must, under this rule, be an independent reason in favor of doing the promised thing, even if, as it turns out, the promising rule is overridden by other rules. But we have argued that it cannot be an independent reason in cases of promising the immoral. There is no good reason why we should do what we have assured others we will do unless *what* we have assured them is a morally proper thing to do. The point is that promising must function as a reason for doing something *in addition* to other considerations, or in spite of them, if the duty of promising keeping is to function as a prima facie duty. But it does not. Promising the immoral is not a reason for doing the immoral that gets defeated because it is immoral. One does not reason that, in promising to kill, the points in favor of the action derived from the promise are defeated by the points against it derived from the killing, or that the killing rule overrides the promising rule but, rather, that the promise in this case has no moral weight at all. The question we are raising, then, is: What moral work does promising do? What does it add to or subtract from other moral considerations?

A relatively recent account of prima facie obligations may help make this clear. Paul M. Pietroski, in "Prima Facie Obligations, Ceteris Paribus Laws in Moral Theory,"[21] claims that the following statement is easily refuted because it is subject to well-known counterexamples:

> If M promises to make some state of affairs s the case, then M ought to perform an action, a, which makes s the case.[22]

By 'ought,' he means an 'actual obligation' as opposed to a prima facie obligation. But he also claims that this view of a promise is analogous to a statement of a physical law:

> If a force, f, impinges on a ball at rest, the ball will move in the direction of f at a velocity, v, where v is a function of the magnitude of and the mass of the ball.[23]

If this law is read as holding "absolutely" it is easy to falsify. Instead, the law should be read as implicitly containing "other things being equal" or "ceteris paribus" (CP) conditions. He goes on to claim:

At a minimum, 'exceptions' to a true CP law must be explicable as the result of some kind of 'interference.' Billiard ball mechanics is not falsified by the mere fact that some particular ball fails to move north in spite of being pushed north. We are, however, committed to there being an explanation for why such a ball fails to move north. Thus, we might say that a CP clause offers a 'promissory note' to the effect that there is a correct explanation for each exception to the lawlike statement it modified. The explanation will typically take the form of citing a further factor, for example, another force impinging on the ball from another direction.[24]

Guided by his examination of CP laws, Pietroski explains prima facie obligations (indicated by the subscript 'pf'):

"M ought$_{pf}$ to do X" is true iff CP, M ought$_{act}$ to do X.

This is then explicitly related to promises:

We can read the English sentence 'Agents ought to keep their promises' as (a) a claim which ascribes prima facie obligations or (b) a claim which ascribes actual obligations but which also contains an implicit CP clause.[25]

As he makes clear,[26] (a) and (b) both come to the same thing. Understood in this reasonable way, we ask whether interpreting promises as prima facie obligations, as Pietroski does, solves the problem we presented above.

Consider how Pietroski would analyze a conflict over promises. He gives an example of Morty who promised he would be at a station on time and also feels an obligation to help a child in need. He concludes that this is really a matter of weighing "relevant forces": "For the *intuitive* answer is surely the right answer in each case: it depends on the relative strength of the relevant forces." We add emphasis to 'intuition' because he previously claimed:

This is not yet to say that composition principles for ethics are waiting to be found. Perhaps the best we can do is to say that 'intuition must decide' how to weight the various CP generalization in various cases.

But perhaps not; and I do not think we have to take a stand on the (hard) question in advance of the investigation.[27]

By compositional principles Pietroski has in mind circumstances (similar those designated by G. E. Moore as "organic unities") where separate actions, each of which may produce an unfavorable outcome individually, can produce a desired effect when combined (or vice versa).

This does not help much to solve the problems we find in promising. Consider his statement of the law involving forces and his claim about promises. Notice an important difference. A force is quantitative. Its quantity explains the direction of change. The power of the force is factored into the statement of the law and serves to resolve the CP conditions. Moreover, Pietroski's initial statement of the rule about promising does not talk about the content of a promise. Promising is supposed to create a prima facie obligation independent of its content. Yet, in his example, Pietroski does not weigh the mere act of promising against other obligations but, in addition, considers the content of the promise. The question he raises is whether being at the station is more important than helping the child in need. If the force of making a promise were the only thing in question, then the conflict would be between keeping a promise and helping the child. Thus, Pietroski's example shifts our attention from the prima facie obligation to keep a promise, *any* promise, to a consideration of the importance of doing the promised thing.

If it is true that the content of the promise and not the promise determines the actual obligation, then the act of promising plays no determinable role in the deliberation. The promise is not doing the moral work of creating an independent prima facie obligation. The promise in itself provides no moral assurance. The supposed moral force of promising gets lost in the analysis. But this is not the way in which most philosophers, including Pietroski, want to think about promises. They really want to claim that a promise creates a prima facie obligation independently of its content.

If a promise creates a prima facie obligation, under the rule that we ought to keep our promises, then the deliberation should focus on whether it is more important to keep a promise than it is to help a child. Thus, Morty may decide to go the station *because he promised*, allowing the prima facie obligation of promise keeping to win out over benevolence, but this is just the sort of reasoning that seems to us so morally objectionable. Doing something of little importance wins out over something of greater importance just because it was promised!

Thus, if the making of a promise has any power at all, aside from its content or the importance of keeping it, there will be cases in which relatively trivial acts will override more serious concerns. The only way to save promising from this criticism, it seems, is to allow all other prima facie moral obligations to override promises. Suppose then we say that promises come last, or are at the very lowest point in our list of prima facie obligations. Would this position avoid the problems we raised?

The matter is rather complex. We know that there is no full agreement on the nature and extent of moral obligations. Suppose a person who holds the view that promise keeping comes last in the list of prima facie obligations believes that he or she has many other obligations. For example, this person might believe that he or she is morally obliged to meet classes on time, to help around the house, to take a hand in raising the kids, to work diligently on research and writing, to be informed about social issues, and to make his or her voice known on several crucially important issues, and so forth. Now, given such beliefs, claiming that promising comes last on the long list of prima facie obligations surely means that his or her promises do not really assure that an action will be done. If the person making the promise made this clear by saying, "I promise to meet with you unless it does not conflict with helping around the house, taking care of the kids, and so on," we would expect the promisee to object, "No, I need a *promise*." But we know, of course, that promises are not made in this way. Moreover, it is doubtful that such a person would be able to list all of his or her prima facie obligations. Instead, he or she is likely to promise without adding the long list of obligations that could nullify keeping the promise.

It is now easy to conclude that in a rich moral world, putting promises last on the list of prima facie obligations won't work. It makes promising practically pointless. It would be much better for such a person to avoid promising altogether, for such promises are bound to mislead.

In a more sparsely populated moral world promises would seem to offer some degree of assurance without trumping other moral values.

Suppose that a person believes that we have very few moral obligations: for example, not to lie, to steal, to kill, or to commit adultery. Let us say that all of these are prima facie duties. And among the short list is the rule, "Keep promises." But promising is the least in importance, or, in the terminology of Pietroski, has the least moral force. Now we can say that reasonable and moral people (who share this view) would not want us to keep promises at the cost of lying, stealing, killing, committing adultery, and so on. So a promise seems like a legitimate conditional assurance, and the conditions may be supposed to be generally known.

But the problem here has to do with the deficiency of such a person's limited moral view. Let's call this person "Sally." Helping her spouse and children are not included on the list of moral obligations. So her promises seem to assure in a more robust way. But suppose that Sally promises something trivial. Remember that the theory we are examining claims that the promise and not the content of the promise creates the moral obligation. Sally's trivial promise now has a prima facie binding force, even though it is last on her short list of prima facie duties. The promise overrides all kinds of prudential obligations, even acts of benevolence, some of which, for most of us, would be considered morally binding. The trivial promise takes precedence over all other goods, even those of great value. If, say, Sally is offered a large amount of money to give a lecture at the time when she is supposed to keep her trivial promise, she must do the trivial thing and give up the money her family badly needs—just because she promised.

Thus, philosophers might try to save promises from moral conflict by putting promises last on the list of prima facie duties and, at the same time, deregulating much of the moral world. But both claims seem unacceptable. Indeed, why would anyone place promises last? Well, it seems, just to avoid the kinds of problems we point out. As a matter of fact, no theorist we know about has explicitly claimed that promises come last on the list. We have merely supposed that they would need to do so in order to meet our objections. Moreover, a short list of moral obligations (like Sally's) probably would not include "Keep your promises." Everyone knows that some and perhaps many promises are about trivial matters, so why include a general duty of promise keeping at all? Well, only because, we believe, the duty of promising keeping is supported by popular wisdom and hallowed by moral and philosophical tradition, but not because it has independent rational support.

As we have seen, the notion of prima facie obligation, at least as it applies to promises, is not well developed. Philosophers who believe that they can save promises, or a duty of promise keeping, merely by claiming that such a duty is prima facie would do well explain how their theory is supposed to work. They may object to our schema by arguing that prima facie obligations cannot be ranked, thinking that actual obligations must be decided on a case by case basis, by moral intuition. But such an answer, we believe, is a retreat into vagueness and indeterminacy, amounting to a refusal to take a stand on the issue. An appeal to intuition is, in fact, an abandonment of reason in ethics, for it is a claim that, in the final analysis, reasons do not and cannot resolve moral issues. That is at least what the act deontologist H. A. Prichard meant when he argued, in favor of intuition, that the rightness or wrongness of an act cannot be demonstrated by any process of reasoning whatsoever.[28] Yet even Prichard thought that we should take reasons into account. The question is then: what role do the reasons play?

If one is an objectivist, or moral realist, as Prichard was, then reasons (or intuitions for that matter) do not really *determine* which acts are right. The reasons are, rather, means of *discovering* acts that are independently right. Moreover, the reasons, or the intuitions, are not infallible in picking out right acts, as Prichard pointed out, for any process of reasoning or intuition might be mistaken. Certainly people who have contradictory intuitions cannot both be right. So according to the intuitionist view, there seems to be no way of discovering who in the final analysis is right, for there are no reasons, or criteria, capable of determining the answers.

Thus, if we accept a final appeal to intuition, we are left with a situation in which, it seems, anybody can claim anything at all without having to justify his or her judgment. Prima facie rules may be said to play a part, but the intuitionist seems unable to explain what part they play. The rules are never sufficient to determine an actual obligation in a particular case. And the theory is not improved by denying objectivism, or by holding that actual obligations are determined by reason, or by reason plus intuition, for there is still no procedure for resolving conflicts. When it comes to promise keeping, there is still no way of knowing when the so-called prima facie duty of promise keeping trumps other moral obligations and when it does not.

Frank Snare, in "The Definition of *Prima Facie* Duties,"[29] examines this issue. He worries whether an intuitionist can specify the extent and power of prima facie obligations. He concludes,

> I do not even think an Intuitionist has to believe that complete knowl-edge of the true moral code is an attainable goal. This might be for two reasons. First, he may never be entirely certain that there is not yet one more *prima facie* duty which he has so far overlooked or failed to intuit. Secondly, even where he knows his *prima facie* duties he may still be unclear in many cases as to what to do in a conflict. . . . There may be a fundamental consensus in some culture on certain *prima facie* duties, but when these come into conflict there may be no thought-out views and rather pervasive confusion.[30]

Confusion involving statements of assurance is hardly a virtue.

We have said that part of the problem is that the duty of promise keeping is confused with the duty to do the promised thing. One might argue that this is not really a confusion because promises do not have an independent but an additive or compositional moral force. That is, one may be tempted to maintain that promising adds to the impor-tance of doing the promised thing. If the promised act is important in itself, then it becomes more important by being promised, and if it is trivial, it becomes less trivial. On this account, a less trivial promise might still be trivial and hence be overridden by a more serious con-cern. The content of the promise would then need to be considered in determining whether the prima facie duty of promise keeping is an actual duty.

However, the results are the same. A serious matter backed by a promise either overrides or does not override a more serious matter that is not promised. If it does, it is still immoral to keep the promise, and if it doesn't, it provides little or no assurance. Either a promise does some moral work and alters our obligations or it does no moral work at all. To say that it does a little moral work, in an additive way, is of no help, and like all other prima facie positions, short changes the whole notion of promising.

The reader is surely growing tired of this. Why keep making the same point over and over again in slightly different ways? The reason we have done so is because philosophers seem willing to go to great lengths to save "the institution of promising." When challenged, or faced with moral conflict, they seem willing to devise all sorts of ad hoc theories to defend their belief. That is why we have attempted to show, in some detail, why none of these theories will work, not even in principle, and certainly not in practice. The inventors of these theories seem to forget that promising is a form of communication, and hence fail to specify what exactly is communicated by it. A promise is a promise, no more, no less. If a theory about promising becomes too esoteric, too convoluted, or too vague, one begins to wonder how anyone may be expected to follow it. According to such theories, how would anyone know what exactly is being assured, or to what extent they can count upon such assurance?

We have challenged our philosophical opponents to explain exactly what difference a promise is supposed to make in moral deliberations, but the reader should notice that we have not denied that promising *can* make a difference. Our main point has been that it is not the act of promising alone that creates a moral obligation, even a prima facie obligation. But a promise can make a difference in moral deliberation, if one considers the content of a promise, or the seriousness of keeping it or not keeping it, relative to other moral demands. This is because, as we shall argue later, a promise can lead a promisee (and perhaps others) to *count upon* its being kept. Thus, a promisor may need to weigh the value of performing a promised act against the value of other alternatives, because of expectation or reliance, in a way that he or she would not need to do so if there were no promise. In this respect, promises are similar to contracts or agreements, for, although contracts and agreements are not explicit assurances, the parties involved may intentionally lead one another to expect performance. Morally speaking, one needs to take account of the reliance created by one's acts, but one does not need to assign to promises, or to agreements or contracts, for that matter, any special obligation-creating power to account for this.

Those who reject our position, we believe, tend to equivocate on this point. They start off talking about promises as obligation-creating acts and end up talking about promises as if they were mere statements of intention or agreements in which any obligation to perform depends, not on the fact that a promise or agreement was made, but upon the importance of doing or not doing the promised or agreed upon thing. They thus tend to confuse the mere act of making a promise with the importance of satisfying the expectation or reliance created by it. Promises often do create such reliance. But they may not, for a promisee may release a promisor from a promise or simply not depend on it. In such cases, there would obviously be no need to weigh the importance of the promisee's reliance on the promise, and hence no obligation to weigh the importance of the promise. Of course, a promised act may be an important thing to do or not do in its own right, but that is a wholly independent matter.

In shifting from the notion that promises are obligation-creating acts to the notion that pormisors have an obligation to consider the effects of their promises upon promisees (and perhaps others), our advocates of promising also keep forgetting that promises are assurances. And, as assurances, promises are deceptive, for they claim to assure what cannot reasonably be assured. This is made especially clear by the claim that promises create prima facie obligations, for the whole point of saying they are prima facie is to say that they are defeasible. That is why we have argued that one simply cannot have it both ways at once. Either promises are assurances or they are not. Either they create an obligation to keep the promise or they do not. The "it-all-depends" responses that have been conjured up to save the so-called duty of promise keeping are simply admissions that promises cannot reasonably be genuine moral assurances. What promises can do is arouse expectations in a hearer, and promisors, we agree, should be held responsible for that.

The truth is that, in promising, people often do know what is being assured, and they know *that* it is being assured. They may, therefore, rely heavily upon the keeping of a promise, as they often do. But, if they are wise, they should also realize that such promises are deceptive, and hence that promises may not be kept, for all sorts of reasons, both moral and immoral. Indeed, the opposing theories considered in this chapter serve to illustrate just how deceptive promises can be.

PARADOXICAL CONSEQUENCES

A paradoxical consequence of these considerations is that the promises of an immoral promisor seem to provide greater assurance than the promises of a moral promisor. This paradox of promising, which appears to have escaped the attention of moral philosophers, casts serious doubt on the justification and efficacy of the practice of promising. The paradox is that, among persons who take promises seriously, those who, in promising, ignore other moral obligations, or who take other obligations less seriously, are likely to be more assuring, or more reliable, than promises made by those who give more weight to other obligations. Since the purpose of promising is to give assurance, more assurance is given by persons who ignore or discount other moral obligations than by those who are sensitive to them.

There is another paradoxical side effect: an immoral promisor is likely to have a greater moral obligation to keep a promise. This is because the promise of such a person is likely to create greater expectation or reliance. We have argued that there is a difference between the morality of making a promise and the morality of keeping a promise. Our view is that reliance is crucial in determining obligations of promise- keeping that follow from immoral acts of making promises. We merely wish to say now that there is nothing odd about claiming that moral obligations follow from immoral acts. If one steals, for example, one may incur moral obligations as a result of the theft.

Theoretically the strength of the assurance of a promise depends on the other obligations it can or cannot justifiably trump. In actual practice, individual promisors may or may not have a particular theory of promising in mind, but they will attach more or less weight to the promises they give. Hence, in particular cases, they will sometimes allow promises to override other obligations and at other times not. If, however, they have a consistent belief system in such matters and act accordingly, or if their actions follow a predictable pattern, the extent to which their promises can be relied upon, or the types of cases in which they can be relied upon, may reasonably be predicted. If so, promisees may be able to determine when and how much they can depend on the keeping of a promise. They will be able to know, even if only roughly, that a person who takes promises very seriously will tend to override or discount other obligations, and a person who takes promises less seriously will tend to override or discount promises. Hence the paradox, not only in theory but also in practice. A person who places O_p high on the list discounts many other obligations. In this sense, the person is immoral. But that person is, other things being equal, a more reliable promisor than one who places O_p lower on the list.

The second paradox closely follows upon the first. The second paradox is that, if the obligation to keep a promise is at all dependent on expectation or reliance, which it certainly seems to be, then the so-called immoral promisor, as we describe such a person, has a greater obligation to keep a promise than a person who takes other obligations more seriously. This is because, if rational, promisees (and others) are likely to place more reliance on the promises of such immoral promisors than on the promises of moral promisors. One might argue that an immoral promisor cannot be obligated to do immoral things: i.e., that the immoral promisor cannot rightly override other obligations, however much he or she may believe that his or her promise can or should do so. But that is just the point. One may try to reform the immoral promisor by convincing him or her to take promises less seriously, but this weakens the assurance promises are supposed to give.

CONCLUSION

If we are correct, the practice of promising should be discarded. Promising is one of those practices that is thought to be morally acceptable, even necessary, but which, upon analysis, is morally wrong. The problems involved in promising are similar to problems associated with other so-called obligations of "honor,"[31] such as those involving revenge, that are now condemned. In the past, honor played a more important role in popular morality than it does today, although in some contexts people still do things because they think honor dictates. The general moral objection to acts of honor is that they conflict with other moral obligations. We propose that promising similarly succumbs to the same objection.

NOTES

1. An earlier version of part of this chapter was published as "The Immorality of Promising," *Journal of Value Inquiry* 27 (1993).

2. Stephen Toulmin asserts that the practice of promising is beyond criticism. *Reason in Ethics* (Cambridge: Cambridge University Press, 1960), p. 150. Oswald Hanfling likewise believes that "it is not clear what sense we could make of . . . questions like 'Is promising a good thing?', 'Ought we to have promising or do away with it?'" "Promises, Games, and Institutions," *Proceedings of the Aristotelian Society* 75 (1974–75): 21.

3. John R. Searle believes that the "essential feature of a promise is that it is the undertaking of an obligation to perform a certain act. I think that this condition distinguishes promises . . . from other kinds of illocutionary acts." *Speech Acts*, p. 60.

4. G. J. Warnock, *The Object of Morality* (London: Methuen, 1971), p. 98.

5. Thomas Scanlon, "Promises and Practices," *Philosophy and Public Affairs* 19 (1990): 208.

6. John Rawls, *A Theory of Justice* (Cambridge, Mass.: Harvard University Press, 1971), p. 346.

7. Michael H. Robins, *Promising, Intending, and Moral Autonomy* (Cambridge: Cambridge University Press, 1984), p. 120.

8. Scanlon, "Promises and Practices," p. 204.

9. Christopher McMahon points out that promises lack the bilateral character of coordination proposals. "Promising and Coordination," *American Philosophical Quarterly* 2 (1989): 245. See also J. P. W. Cartwright, "An Evidentiary Theory of Promises," *Mind* 93 (1984): 235.

10. Paul Ardal, "And That's a Promise," *Philosophical Quarterly* 18 (1968): 225.

11. We assume here but argue elsewhere that it is possible to make agreements without actually promising to keep them.

12. Many may object to such a list as beyond our moral knowledge, or as being too inflexible. Neither objection should hamper the reading of the promisor's paradox. First of all, the list is meant as an ordering that could be

made, given full knowledge. We assume the list would be quite long, and not within our ability to fully state. The list need not be inflexible. Assuming a very long list, or an infinitely long list, that may involve compound obligations, and obligations depending on the seriousness of the issues at hand, all the arguments made in our text continue to hold. In short, we offer the list as heuristically helpful in coming to grips with the issues involved in promising. No more is intended.

13. Daniel Kading, "On Promising without Moral Risk," *Philosophical Studies* 11 (1960): 55.

14. Ibid., pp. 58–59.

15. Ibid., p.58.

16. Ibid., p.59.

17. Ibid., p.60.

18. Ibid.

19. Ibid.

20. W. D. Ross, *The Right and the Good* (Oxford: The Clarendon Press, 1930), pp. 19–20.

21. Paul M. Pietroski, "Prima Facie Obligations, Ceteris Paribus Laws in Moral Theory," *Ethics* 103 (1993): 489–515.

22. Ibid., p. 495.

23. Ibid., p. 496.

24. Ibid., pp. 495–96.

25. Ibid., p. 497.

26. Ibid., p. 501.

27. Ibid., p. 502.

28. H. A. Prichard, "Does Moral Philosophy Rest on a Mistake," *Mind* 21 (1912).

29. Frank Snare, "The Definition of *Prima Facie* Duties," *Philosophical Quarterly* 24 (1974).

30. Ibid., p. 236.

31. R. S. Downie, "Three Accounts of Promising," *Philosophical Quarterly* 35 (1985): 269.

five

ON MAKING AND KEEPING PROMISES

The man who promises everything is sure to fulfil nothing, and everyone who promises too much is in danger of using evil means in order to carry out his promises, and is already on the road to perdition.

Carl Jung

In applying their theories to promising (or in attempting to develop theories that can account for obligations of promise keeping) philosophers have usually assumed two things: that there is a general duty to keep promises and that, at least in unusual cases, there are exceptions to this rule. Then, in order to account for the difference between cases that are and are not exceptions to the rule, they have often focused on conditions that must be met at the time of making a promise, instead of focusing on conditions that must be met at the time of keeping a promise. We argue that the relationship between making a promise and the obligation to keep a promise is broken in two ways: (1) a promise may meet one or more of the supposed necessary conditions of promise making and not be obligatory, and (2) an act may be obligatory even if it fails to meet those conditions. That is, not only is no set of conditions of promise making sufficient to establish a moral

95

obligation of promise keeping, but no set of conditions is necessary either. Through our examination of many of the supposed conditions of promise making, we show that the obligation to keep a promise does not depend on conditions that must be satisfied at the time of promise making but, rather, on conditions that must be met at the time of promise keeping. Thus, in this sense, philosophers have been mistaken in focusing their attention on the validity or justification of the act of promising instead of focusing their attention on the justification of the promised act.

Conditions that are supposed to be necessary in order for a promise to be morally binding fall into two categories: (1) conditions at the time a promise is made and (2) conditions at the time the promise is supposed to be kept. Since a promise is typically thought to create a moral obligation, or at least a prima facie obligation, emphasis has been placed on (1), conditions that must be met at the time of making a promise. Under (1) conditions have been laid down for (a) *valid or genuine promises*, as distinct from acts which may appear to be promises but are really not promises, and also for (b) *morally justified promises*, as distinct from promises that are morally wrong. J. E. J. Altham summarizes many of the conditions that fall under (a) and (b), pointing out that philosophers usually concentrate on what he calls the "central cases."

> Central cases are those where the promisor, in full possession of all relevant information and subject to no undue pressure, sincerely promises to perform some action which, independently of the promise, it is perfectly all right for him to perform, and where the promisee, also in full possession of all relevant information and subject to no undue pressure, sincerely accepts the promise. In a central case, no force, fraud, mistake or duress is involved, and the promise is not one to do something that, independently of the promise, one ought not to do.[2]

Altham's list includes both *moral* constraints and *formal* conditions, although he does not distinguish between the two. Force, fraud, and duress certainly appear to be types of morally relevant behaviour, but Altham also mentions conditions that are not clearly moral considerations, such as the promisor's or promisee's being in full possession of all relevant information, or the promisee's sincere acceptance of the promise. The latter appear to be conditions that must be met in order for an act to be a promise, or a valid or genuine promise, as distinct from being a moral or immoral promise. However this distinction is cut, it seems obvious that no act can be a moral or immoral promise unless it is a (valid) promise.

The list of proposed conditions can be expanded. Georg Henrik Von Wright claims that "a promise cannot be performed solo," that a promise must be given and received voluntarily, that the parties must "know what they are doing," that the promisor must be able to perform the *kind* of act promised, and that the "object of the promise must represent an *interest* to the promisee, must be *for him a good*, something he *wants* or *welcomes*."[3] Several authors, including Thomas Scanlon, mention voluntariness on the part of the promisor as a condition of valid or genuine promising. Scanlon adds that the promisee must know of the promise and want it, that the promisor must intend to provide assurance, and that the promisee must know this.[4] Both Scanlon and Von Wright also distinguish between valid promises and moral promises. Von Wright, for example, maintains that "the act of promising to do the forbidden is, for reasons of (deontic) logic, itself a forbidden action."[5] He does not hold that immoral promises are invalid or nongenuine promises but, instead, promises that it would be morally wrong to make. Another type of immoral promise is a lying promise, as referred to by Kant in section 2 of the *Groundwork of the Metaphysics of Morals*.[6] Scanlon refers to Kant when he says, "creating this expectation in others with the intention of disappointing it is wrong."[7]

However, it is not always clear which type of condition philosophers have in mind. For example, when rule-utilitarians or social contractarians speak of social rules or practices as determinants of obligations or duties to keep promises, it is not always clear whether they are speaking in sense (a) or sense (b): whether they mean that there could be no *acts* of promising without subordinate rules or practices, or whether there could be no distinction between justified or unjustified promises. When Rawls, in his "Two Concepts of Rules," distinguishes between summary rules and practice rules, he says of practice rules that they *define* a practice, appearing to mean that such rules determine, in the case of promising, what is or is not a promise.[8] But he also appears to conflate the notion of an act's being a promise with the notion of its *being a justified promise*, or perhaps even more forcefully, *a promise which ought to be kept*. Perhaps separate rules perform these separate functions, but it is a mistake to believe that they all *define* the practice, for some of them would need to *regulate* acts so defined. It is implausible that rules which define a promise also determine whether or not it is justified, or whether or not it ought to be kept. No matter how well established a practice is, some promises are not justified, and not all promises ought to be kept.

This brings us, then, to category (2), namely, conditions that must be met at the time a promised act is to be performed. Even if we allow that the satisfaction of conditions under (1a) and (1b) is necessary to create a moral obligation, the satisfaction of such conditions is not sufficient. That is, allowing that there is a moral principle or rule which says that we ought to keep promises that are both valid and justified, there may still be exceptions in particular cases. This is partly because conditions may arise *after* a promise has been made that would nullify any duty or obligation to keep it. Keeping a promise may, for instance, conflict with some overriding duty or obligation, or keeping one promise may conflict with keeping another, which is why W. D. Ross dubbed the duty to keep promises a prima facie duty.[9] Indeed, an act thought to be possible at the time it is promised may subsequently turn out to be impossible to perform, even if, as Von Wright says, it is an act of a *kind* that it is possible to perform. So an adequate theory of promising needs more than a statement of conditions which determine whether acts are (valid) promises or justified promises: it also needs to determine under what conditions the keeping of promises is or is not obligatory.

In making these distinctions, we wish to consider not only "central" or "ideal" cases, or cases that satisfy conditions laid down by philosophers, but also what we have previously called "degenerate cases,"[10] or what Altham has called "peripheral cases"[11] (i.e., cases thought to be invalid or immoral), in order to determine whether the specified conditions are indeed necessary for the validity or justification of promises and, in any case, whether they must be met in order for promises to be morally binding. These are separate points, for it may be correct to hold that a certain condition must be met in order for a promise to be morally justified, say, but wrong in holding that only morally justified promises are morally binding. Although it appears correct that there can be no obligation to keep a promise unless a (valid) promise has been made, the stated conditions of valid or genuine promising may be incorrect. Some cases, we shall point out, may be clearly degenerate, in either sense (1a) or (1b), or only marginally degenerate in these senses, or they may fail to satisfy some of the conditions mentioned but not all of them, or they may satisfy the conditions in various degrees. By looking at so-called degenerate or peripheral cases, we can ask ourselves whether these should be counted or discounted as valid or justified promises, and how the answer affects the obligation or duty to keep them.

IMMORAL PROMISES

Are immoral promises always nonbinding or wrong to keep? The types of immoral promises usually mentioned by philosophers are lying promises and promises to do things that are immoral. In the case of a lying promise, the promisor does not intend to keep the promise or intends to deceive, and therefore creates a false expectation by convincing the promisee to accept the lie. Well, it certainly seems to be the case that such promises are frequently *made* to win favors or profits, to yield to pressure, or to make others feel better by giving them assurances. A salesperson promises early delivery of a car that he or she believes cannot be kept. In this case, the promise is a lie because the promisor believes that the promised act cannot be done; in other cases, the act is thought possible, but the promisor does not intend to do it. Promisees may be deceived if they believe that an impossible or highly improbable act is possible, or if they believe that the promisor fully intends to perform the act and can be relied upon to do it. A lying promise may therefore succeed in creating reliance, but it need not.

Supposing that such promises are wrong to make, are they wrong to keep? Not necessarily. Indeed, there are reasons for thinking they may good to keep, and that they may even be obligatory. In the case of the salesperson, suppose it turns out that the car could be delivered when promised, despite the salesperson's believing it could not. It seems it would be *good* to deliver the car when promised, and even that it *ought* to be delivered, *because it was promised,* and especially if the promisee relied upon the promise. After all, *it was a promise,* even though a lying promise. The point is that the obligation to keep a promise is not nullified by its being a lying promise, for keeping a lying promise may be a very good or even obligatory thing to do.

Cases in which persons promise to do things that are immoral are different, assuming that the persons who make them are sincere. Obviously, a person could lie in making an immoral promise, by threatening to do bodily harm to another, for example, but also by not intending to carry out the threat. However, we are here concerned with persons who sincerely promise to do immoral things, or at least things which they or others *believe* are immoral, and it certainly seems to be the case that, for this reason, they ought not to keep such promises. Indeed, the claim that promises to do immoral things ought not to be kept seems like a truism, until one notices that it masks an ambiguity. The ambiguity lies in confusing beliefs about the morality or immorality of a promised act at the time a promise is made with the actual morality or immorality of the act at the time it is (or would be) performed. Obviously, an act which is *thought* to be wrong at the time it is promised may actually *be* wrong at the time it is or would be performed, but it may also be *thought wrong* and *be right.* For even if it is a *kind* of act which is as a rule either right or wrong, the particular act which is an instance of that kind may be an exception.

One might argue that it is only acts that are actually wrong that it is wrong to promise, but this rule would be extremely difficult to follow, for it is difficult to know, at the time of promising, which acts will be right or wrong at some future date. The upshot, then, is that persons who promise to do what they or others *think* are immoral acts are not necessarily relieved of the obligation, or are thereby prohibited from doing what they have promised. Thus, the making of a morally justified promise is *not* a necessary condition for the creation of an obligation of promise keeping.

This leads to the question of whether lying promises or promises to do the immoral are always or necessarily unjustified promises. For even if we were to allow that unjustified promises need not or ought not be kept, there is still a question of whether these types of promises are always unjustified. That is, is it always wrong to make a lying promise, or is it always wrong to promise to do something immoral? We have already indicated that a promise may fall under both heads, for a person may promise the immoral but do so by lying. This would seem to make it doubly wrong, but, in point of fact, the lie in this case seems to mitigate the offense. If one promises the immoral, it seems *better* if one does not really intend to keep the promise. Moreover, independently of making promises, it seems that people are sometimes justified in telling lies, so they may sometimes be justified in making lying promises. Are parents wrong in promising or assuring small children that they will always take care of them? Would a prisoner of war be wrong in assuring an enemy that incorrect information about allied positions is in fact correct? If there are such things as beneficent lies, then it would seem that there can be beneficent lying promises as well.

INVALID PROMISES

The conditions held to be necessary for *valid* or *genuine* promise making are more numerous than those thought to be necessary for *justified* promise making, although, as we have said, it is not always clear which conditions are supposed to fall under one or the other of these categories. Von Wright, for example, claims that a valid promise must be of a *kind* that it is possible to perform, but we have already noted that promising the impossible may be an instance of an *immoral* promise and not an instance of an *invalid* promise, if the promisor promises something of a kind he or she knows or believes to be impossible. That would be a lying promise. Von Wright may have in mind the point that a person could not be obligated to *do* an act of a kind that is impossible, but it is difficult to understand why one could not promise such an act, by believing it is possible, or by believing it is impossible and lying. It may be impossible to eliminate the national debt and balance the budget without doing serious damage to the economy, but there is no good reason why politicians cannot promise to do so, as, of course, they do. Likewise, sincerity may be considered a condition of valid promise making, for a person who makes a promise jokingly, say, may be said not to have really promised at all. On the other hand, a person who lies in promising may also be said to be insincere, but such a person would be guilty of making an immoral promise and not an invalid one.

In any case, some of the conditions supposed to be necessary for valid promise-making do not seem to be really necessary. Consider voluntariness. People are frequently coerced into making promises that are certainly *taken to be genuine* by both the promisors and the promisees. Altham claims that "some promises made under duress do bind the promisor. There can be no general doctrine that only a freely made promise binds, and hence that only a freely made promise is really a promise."[12] Let us suppose, for example, that a judge requires a deadbeat dad to make child support payments and the dad is released on the condition that he promises to make such payments. He makes the promise willingly but grudgingly. We are not here concerned with whether he is sincere but with whether his promise is voluntary. One may certainly argue that his promise is voluntary if he makes it willingly, but one might also argue that it is not voluntary on grounds of coercion. If coercion is meant as a disqualifying condition, then in this sense the promise is not freely made. But people are often coerced into making promises, and there would seem to be no point in coercing them if coerced promises were not really promises.[13] Whether or not they are obligated to keep such promises is of course another point. In this case, one might argue that the promised act is obligatory, according to law, even if no promise were made, but, by promising, the deadbeat dad assures the judge that he *will* do what the law requires.

Some of the conditions mentioned refer to the welfare, attitude, or understanding of the promisee. Again, Von Wright says that the thing promised must represent or be a good for the promisee, and if this were so, it seems there could be no valid threats. Generally speaking, threats are promises to do things to people which are not goods but harms, things which are not in their interest, or things they do not want. But, obviously, people do make such promises, and promisees are indeed frequently threatened by them. Again, the point seems to be that, generally speaking, there is no obligation to keep such promises—and it may be the case that it is usually wrong to keep them—but it is quite another thing to say that they are not genuine or valid promises. Thus, the claim that the promisee "must sincerely accept the promise" is ambiguous, for the promisee may accept the fact that it *is* a promise but not at all accept the thought of having the promise fulfilled.

The conditions that are said to be necessary for valid promise making also mention a kind of mutual understanding between the promisor and promisee. It is said that they must both understand what is agreed to in making and accepting the promise, that the promisee must really intend to provide assurance, and the promisee, as above, must want the thing assured. But promises are frequently made in cases where there is no clear understanding of what is being promised, or of what exactly would count as keeping the promise. If a husband promises his wife he will do the dishes, he may discover that his view of completing this task is different from hers: she may not think the promise has been kept until he has cleaned the sink and stove. But even when there is such misunderstanding, it seems improper to conclude that *nothing* was promised, or that no genuine or valid promise was made. Indeed, persons do sometimes make promises *solo*, with no understanding whatsoever on the part of the promisee, since the promisee may not even know that a promise was made. In this case, one may not be required to keep the promise, because, perhaps, there is no expectation or reliance, but the question at issue is whether such a promise really is a promise.

It is possible for a misunderstanding to exist because a promisee takes something to be a promise which the promisor did not intend to be a promise, and this is partly because the objective signs of promising are not always clear. Even when a person says, "I promise," he or she may do so in jest, or as an example, while another person may interpret the saying as serious, or as a matter of direct speech. Of course, other words or signs may be intended or taken to be indicators of promises such as "You have my word" or "I will do it; I said I would." Sometimes the simple saying that one will do something is construed as a promise, and sometimes not. Suppose, then, someone interprets an act to be a promise that is not intended to be a promise, and hence relies on it. In this type of case, one would seem to be correct in holding that no promise was actually made, on the grounds that it was not intended, and hence that there could be no obligation. At least there could be no obligation to perform the act (that was thought to be promised) *because it was promised*, although there might be an obligation to perform it for some other reason (because, say, of the harm of disappointing the expectation or reliance).

The usual evidence for thinking a promise has been made is that someone has used the words "I promise," or some equivalent, in direct speech, and such evidence is usually thought to be *sufficient* for determining that a promise has been made. Hearers naturally and correctly assume that persons who say "I promise" in direct speech intend to give assurance by so saying. That is because, apparently, the function or meaning of the words "I promise" is to give someone assurance. Indeed, the saying of the words "I promise" is sometimes said to be a performative utterance, the saying of which, in direct speech, *constitutes* the making of a promise. If so, it would seem that a person could not use these words intentionally, knowing what they mean, without intending to make a promise.

However, a person may intentionally use the words "I promise," even in direct speech, without being sincere in using them. So a person may, it seems, intentionally use the words "I promise" without intending to make a promise. When challenged, such a person may even claim to have lied in saying "I promise," explaining that he or she meant to give the *appearance* of promising without sincerely intending to make a promise at all. How is this possible, if the saying of the words "I promise" really is a performative utterance and the saying of the words really does constitute promising?

The answer, it seems, lies in making a distinction between the intention to make a promise and the intention to keep it. A person who lies in making a promise by intentionally using the words "I promise" really does intentionally *assure* someone that he or she will do what is promised; otherwise the lie could not succeed in doing what the lie is intended to do. What is being lied about is not the intention of *giving* assurance but the intention of *doing* what is assured. That is why philosophers often speak of lies about *keeping* promises but never, to our knowledge, of lies about *making* them. Thus, a person who intentionally says "I promise" does in fact promise, even if that person does not intend to make a promise in the sense of intending to keep it.

THE PRACTICE VIEW

The idea that promises are performative utterances is often tied to the idea that the conditions of valid and justified promise making, as well as the conditions of obligatory promise keeping, are mandated by social rules, practices, or institutions. Although one would assume that, on a rule view or practice view of promising, rules or practices are needed to determine whether the making or keeping of promises is morally right or wrong, advocates of such views sometimes also seem to believe that the making of *valid* promises also depends on the existence of social practices. For example, Hume,[14] Rawls,[15] and Searle[16] all seem to assume that a valid promise depends on the existence of a well-defined practice, and they also seem to believe that such a practice does indeed exist. But others have rejected these views. Annette Baier, for instance, argues that the conditions referred to by Hume no longer exist,[17] and Stanley Cavell takes issue with Rawls, claiming that there is no practice of promising.[18] Moreover, Scanlon argues, against Rawls, that the obligation to keep promises does not require a social practice, and one would assume from his analysis that he does not think the making of promises requires a social practice either. Scanlon allows that, although the obligation to keep promises is not "generated" by a social practice, promising may *be* a social practice, at least in a limited "linguistic" sense. He says, "It is natural to suppose that the conditions and limitations are 'rules' of the practice of promising," that "by saying 'I promise to . . .' is like renting your house by filling in a preprinted lease form." But he goes on to conclude:

> But while a social practice of agreement-making *could* shape the content of particular obligations arising under it in this way, I am unable to identify any such limitations built into our particular practice of promising. The 'printed form' that it provides appears to be nearly blank.[19]

Thus, if we assume, according to the one view, that there could be no valid promises without an existing practice, and also, according to the other view, that there is no such practice, it follows that there are no valid promises. However, in ordinary life, promises continue to be made, and they also seem to create obligations. If so, one or another of the above- mentioned philosophic claims must be false: either a practice is not required or such a practice does indeed exist.

It is also possible of course that some sort of practice is necessary and does exist—perhaps even more than one—but that it is not the kind of practice described by philosophers. After Baier points out that Hume's account of the practice of promising focuses on a communal willingness to withhold trust from people who fail to keep their promises, she claims that, under Hume's account, in large modern societies the need for promises has been superseded by contracts that are enforced by courts.[20] "The account [Hume] gives us in the *Treatise* is not an account of what becomes of promises once there are magistrates, but of what it can be without them. Once the full panoply of the law is there, everything is changed by its presence."[21] The ability to withhold trust, she maintains, is no longer effective, because of the size of communities and lack of communication. But she also believes there are still promises that are "recognizably Humean" in nature, and that there is an existing practice of promising, different from but similar to the conditions specified by Hume.[22] Unfortunately, she does not specify what this new practice is or how it is supposed to work. The question is whether promises made according to the existing practice are valid, because it *is* the practice, or whether such promises are somehow degenerate, because the existing practice falls short of the type of practice considered necessary by Hume, or by other philosophers who subscribe to the practice view.

It is, of course, difficult to show whether a practice is or is not required for valid promise making, partly because the word "practice" is ambiguous, and there are no generally accepted and well-defined criteria for determining whether a practice does or does not exist. The mere fact that philosophers cannot agree about whether or not a practice of promising exists, even after careful examination, indicates either that they are not all talking about the same thing or that the thing they are looking for is not easy to find.

The practice of promising is difficult to find, we maintain, because no such practice exists. It is our position that a well-defined practice of promising is not necessary and does not exist, simply because, as we have shown, promises are made and do sometimes create obligations, even when the conditions of valid promise making, supposedly laid down by social practices, are violated. Practices can be created, as they have been in contract law, specifying conditions that must be met in order for a contract to be *legally* binding, but, as Baier points out, contract law does not constrain the promises of private life. Perhaps one of the reasons why philosophers have supposed that promising is governed by a well-defined institution or practice is that they have confused promises with contracts, as even Hume appears to have done. Hume appears to conflate the idea of promising with that of contracts in his chapter "Of Morals" in the *Treatise*. There are many other examples. Atiyah argues, as we do, that many of the claims of philosophers about the conditions of valid promising are false, but he does so by assimilating the idea of making a promise with that of making a legal contract.[23] Katharine Bath closely relates promises and contracts; for her, the rules of contract law apply to promises and "give the meaning of promises."[24] Furthermore, "promises may differ slightly in different societies; for there will be cross-cultural variations in the legal rules relating to promises."[25]

Another apparent reason is that, in recent history, some philosophers have become enamored of game analogies, thinking that the rules of morality are like the rules of games. Thus, when Rawls, for example, argues that practice rules *define* a practice, he has in mind the idea that the rules of a game define correct moves within that game, that the objects of games and the moves within them are *created by the rules*. But, as we have tried to show, when it comes to promising, no special rules are required. All that is needed is the saying of the words "I promise," or the use of some other sign or signs indicating that an assurance of something is being given to someone. Such signs may require linguistic conventions, so that persons may know what is meant by them, but they do not require social rules or institutions.

THE GENERAL CONFUSION

More importantly, however, the mistakes philosophers have made in specifying the conditions of valid promise making are, as G. E. Moore has said, a result of not being clear about the questions they are trying to answer. In general, they have confused questions of promise making with questions of promise keeping. And they have done this by supposing that the conditions that must be met in order for a promise to be morally binding are also the conditions that must be met in order for a promise to be valid. For example, P. S. Atiyah writes, "To a lawyer at least, it would seem clear that the only purpose of trying to decide whether a statement is a promise is to decide whether the statement carries an obligation with it."[26] If they would keep in mind that these are separate issues, they could treat the matter of making promises separately from questions about keeping them. They have found it difficult to do this, it seems, because they have continued to believe that the making of promises can somehow magically create obligations. Since, however, they have realized that not all promises can create obligations, they have tried to locate the difference between those that do and those that do not in the promises themselves, or in the kinds of promises they are, instead of focusing on the conditions of obligatoriness that must be met at the time of keeping a promise. For example, Scanlon writes, "Saying 'I promise to . . .' normally binds one to do the thing promised, but it does not bind unconditionally or absolutely. It does not bind unconditionally because the binding force of promising depends on the conditions under which the promise is made."[27]

No promise, no matter how pristine, can by itself create any obligation, for it does not follow from the fact that one intends to take on an obligation by promising that one therefore has that obligation, even if all of the conditions of promising, laid down by philosophers, should happen to be met. The important question, therefore, is what conditions must be met at the time of keeping a promise, in order for a promised act to be morally justified or obligatory. This question can be answered, it seems, only by applying moral principles and rules to the promised act, as to any other act. The only difference appears to be that a promise can create expectation or reliance that might not have been created if there were no promise. This expectation or reliance is certainly a factor to be taken into consideration in determining moral obligation, but it is not the only factor, nor is it necessarily a decisive one.

NOTES

1. This chapter is a slightly modified version of "On Making and Keeping Promises," *Journal of Applied Ethics* 13 no. 2 (1996).

2. J. E. J. Altham, "Wicked Promises," in *Exercises in Analysis,* ed. I. Hacking (Cambridge: Cambridge University Press, 1985), p. 1.

3. Georg Hendrick Von Wright, "On Promises," *Practical Reason*, Philosophical Papers, vol. 1 (Ithaca, N.Y.: Cornell University Press, 1983), pp. 83–87.

4. Thomas Scanlon, "Promises and Practices," *Philosophy and Public Affairs* 19 (1990): 208.

5. Von Wright, "On Promises," p. 95.

6. Kant, *Groundwork of the Metaphysics of Morals,* sect. 2.

7. Scanlon, "Promises and Practices," p. 203.

8. John Rawls, "Two Concepts of Rules," *Philosophical Review* 64 (1955): 3–32.

9. W. D. Ross, *The Right and the Good* (Oxford: The Clarendon Press, 1930).

10. J. P. DeMarco and R. M. Fox, "Putting Pressure on Promises," *Southern Journal of Philosophy* 30 (1992): 45–58.

11. Altham, "Wicked Promises," p. 1.

12. Ibid., p. 10.

13. Thomas Hobbes claims that a promise binds even though coerced by a robber on the threat of death. *De Cive* (Molesworth, 1839), chap. 2, sec. 16, p. 58. See also Louis Marinoff, "Hobbes, Spinoza, Kant, Highway Robbery and Game Theory," *Australasian Journal of Philosophy* 72 (1994): 445–62.

14. David Hume, "Of Morals," in *A Treatise of Human Nature,* 2d. ed., ed. P. H. Nidditch (Oxford: The Clarendon Press, 1978), pp. 516–25.

15. Rawls, "Two Concepts of Rules."

16. John Searle, *Speech Acts: An Essay in the Philosophy of Language* (London: Cambridge University Press, 1969).

17. Baier believes that Hume's position depends on the existence of a small community in which a reputation for breaking promises quickly spreads. Annette Baier, "Promises, Promises, Promises," chap. 10 in *Postures of the Mind: Essays on Mind and Morals* (Minneapolis: University of Minnesota Press), pp. 174–204.

18. Stanley Cavell, "Rules and Reasons," chap. 11 in *The Claim of Reason: Wittgenstein, Skepticism, Morality, and Tragedy* (New York: Oxford University Press, 1979), pp. 292–312.

19. Scanlon, "Promises and Practices," pp. 214–16.

20. Baier, "Promises, Promises, Promises," p. 188.

21. Ibid., p. 203.

22. Ibid., p. 204.

23. P. S. Atiyah, "Promises and the Law of Contract."

24. Katharine Bath, "Promises and Assertions," *Philosophia* 8 (1978): 531.

25. Ibid., p. 521.

26. Atiyah , "Promises and the Law of Contract," p. 414.

27. Scanlon, "Promises and Practices," p. 214.

six

CONTRACTS
AND PROMISES

Promises are the uniquely human way of ordering the future, making it predictable and reliable to the extent that this is humanly possible.

Hannah Arendt

Promising is said to be an important social practice because it is a way—perhaps even the best way—of assuring the performance of future actions. Without promises, presumably, persons would be less effective in planning their lives. In a complex society, where individuals depend on one another in countless ways, promises are considered a needed way to elicit mutually supportive behavior. But, obviously, promises are not the only way. Statements of intention, agreements, contracts, customs, laws, habits, and even self-interest are all bases for predictions about the future actions of others, providing grounds for reasonable expectation and reliance.

Promises may serve as a basis for prediction, but we have argued that, while promises profess to give strong assurance, they cannot really guarantee performance. Since people often fail to keep their promises, for both good and bad reasons, promising appears to offer no more assurance of performance than other ways of establishing expectation.

Indeed, some foundations for prediction, or reliance, such as contracts, may be better than promises in this respect, for, unlike promises, contracts are backed by institutional rules and sanctions, as promises are sometimes mistakenly thought to be.

Contracts are of special interest as an alternative to promises because they may provide better assurance without the intention of creating a special moral obligation to perform. But whether contracts are a genuine alternative depends on their independence from promising. Some theorists have claimed that contracts derive their force from promises, or that contracts just are promises backed by law, or even, conversely, that promises themselves are best understood as contracts. Thus, to be an alternative to promises, it must be shown that contracts are distinct. One of the ways in which they are distinct, as just mentioned, is that contracts do have institutional backing in a way that promises do not. We shall also show that contracts, unlike promises, are not deceptive, misleading, or morally improper assurances of performance, as promises are. For this reason, contracts are not saddled with the problem of creating the appearance of assuring what cannot reasonably be assured.

Legal enforcement gives to contracts a predictive force that promises do not have. Contracts are usually much clearer and more detailed than promises in listing the terms of agreement and in certifying a meeting of minds. Statutes place prior restrictions on the terms of contracts, while there are no explicit (if any) rules governing the conditions or contents of valid or actionable promises. The legal adjudication of contract disputes also adds to the determination of contractual obligations an element of fairness not part of the practice of promising. In these ways contracts avoid many of the objectionable features of promises previously explored: exploitation, vagness, and misunderstanding.

Although decisions of courts in cases of contract law are far from consistent, there are explicit rules governing contracts that can be identified, and these can be interpreted or amended according to legal principles and precedents. In fact, major changes in contract law over the years reveal that contract law has moved away from the more traditional promising model of interpretation to a model based on legal principles and statutes: the very kind of change, we have contended, that is demanded by morality; i.e., the abandonment of promise making and strict adherence to promises in deference to moral principles and rules.

CONTRACTS AS PROMISES

The word "promise" is given a prominent place in textbook definitions of contracts. The *Restatement of Contracts* asserts, "A contract is a promise or a set of promises for the breach of which the law gives a remedy, or the performance of which the law in some way recognizes as a duty."[1] In keeping with this definition, Charles Fried claims, in his theory of contracts as promises, that a view of contracts as dependent on the moral authority of promises best explains, predicts, and guides the behavior of courts.[2] Fried rejects the "death-of-contract" position: namely, the view that contract law is in the process of being replaced by the law of torts and that contract disputes should be settled on grounds of fairness.

In 1974, G. Gilmore published *The Death of Contract*, in which he proclaims:

> We may take the fact that damages in contract have become indistinguishable from damages in tort as obscurely reflecting an instinctive, almost unconscious realization that the two fields, which had been artificially set apart, are gradually merging and becoming one.[3]

Gilmore argues that, in the past, contracts were interpreted to be an instrument of turn-of-the-century, individualistic, free-market capitalism, but that this is no longer the case. However, Fried, in opposition to Gilmore, contends that freely made promises are still the moral basis of contract law.

Vincent A. Wellman points out that Fried revives the notion of a contract as a meeting of the minds used to express voluntary agreement. This Wellman labels the "subjective" or "will" theory of contracts.

> The will theory seems to have been more prominent over a century ago. . . . But, the will theory fell from favor thereafter, and contract scholars shifted from an individualistic understanding of contractual

liability to a view of contract that is sometimes referred to as an objective theory. On this latter view, the appropriate basis for imposing contractual liability was held to be the needs of society for an efficient and reliable regime of enforceable transactions.[4]

Gilmore observes that hard cases required a closer and revised analysis of the court's role in adjudicating contracts. Suppose, for example, that a firm acting in good faith expects a contract and produces goods based on precontract requests. The firm may need to be compensated for losses if no purchase is made, even if no contract is written. In the face of such problems, and others involving fairness, courts have made decisions that do not require explicit contractual agreements. In this way courts have clearly extended the notion of a contract beyond the constraints of promises. On the enforcement side, the courts have often considered a nonbreaching party's reliance and the actual harm caused by reliance upon the contract instead of granting what would have been gained without the breach.[5] In this way courts apply standards of fairness that do not conform to the terms of the original agreement.

Fried criticizes decisions imposing an independent standard as violations of the rights of people to freely commit themselves to cooperative endeavors without having external requirements forced upon them. Settlements, when required, should be made in terms of the original contract. People have a right to invoke, he believes, the already established convention of promising, and they should then keep, and courts should respect, the promsises made. On his view, a promise does not merely invite reliance:

> We need to isolate an additional element, over and above benefit, reliance, and communication of intention. That additional element must *commit* me, and commit me to more than the truth of some statement.[6]

According to Fried, a contract is not merely a true statement of intention: it also involves an obligation, a moral obligation, to perform. For Fried, this element of commitment comes directly from the moral authority of promises.

Fried believes that contracts are needed to cement the assurances given by promises because self-interest may prove hostile to moral commitment. The coercive power of the law rightly sanctions promises made through contracts precisely because such promises are freely made and morally binding:

> If I make a promise to you, I should do as I promise; and if I fail to keep my promise, it is fair that I should be made to hand over the equivalent of the promised performance."[7]

Thus, in considering damages for breach, he proposes that people actually receive what they bargain for or its equivalence.

Fried bases his notion of the moral power of promises, and hence contracts, on autonomy and trust. Such personal expressions of freedom, he holds, ought to be respected. Without trust, we could not assume that another person's commitment would assure future performance. Fried believes that those who see contract law as a way to avoid harm caused by breach—those who do not insist on equivalent performance—fail to take seriously the promisor as a autonomous moral person. Nevertheless, Fried agrees that sometimes equivalent value of performance cannot be determined; in such cases, harm done may be used as a proxy to measure equivalent value.[8]

The theory of contracts as promises runs into some of the difficulties we have previously explored, involving, for example, determination of the existence of a valid promise and its full meaning. We argued that differences of opinion about whether a valid promise exists can undermine the intended purpose of a promise, namely to assure the performance of a course of action. Fried recognizes such problems about the validity of contracts and offers his own views about the conditions under which a valid contract is made:

> I have made or implied a number of qualifications to my thesis. The promise must be freely made and not unfair. . . . It must also have been made rationally, deliberately. The promisor must have been serious enough that subsequent legal enforcement was an aspect of what he should have contemplated at the time he promised. Finally, certain promises, particularly those affecting the situation and expec-

tations of various family members, may require substantive regulation because of the legitimate interests of third parties.[9]

This set of requirements, of course, is far from clearly formed. "Unfairness" is not a concept that can be glibly thrown into discussion. His stipulation that legal enforcement is reasonably foreseen by the promisor adds a requirement extrinsic to the contract, as does the requirement that certain interests of family should be protected. One of the problems with theories of promising, as we have pointed out, is that philosophers claim there is a social convention of promising in place but then speculate on the rules and requirements of that convention. This seems to be what Fried is doing. He invokes the convention of promising and then informs us about how that convention is structured and related to contracts; this suggests that the convention requires his specifications. As it stands, the "convention of promising" is too amorphous to support his strong reliance on it.

Fried expects his theory to explain, predict and guide behavior of courts; after all, a contract is a legal matter. It is thus appropriate to test his view by contract adjudication. On his theory, we would expect courts to enforce most contracts as agreed upon, using the notion of specific performance, requiring the contracted actions or equivalent performance where specific performance is not possible. Thus, if unforeseen events occur which make it reasonable for one person to breach the contract, under Fried's promise view, such breach is to be discouraged by enforcing specific or equivalent performance. Yet courts seldom require specific performance and often use standards different from equivalent performance. Furthermore, if courts did act in the way Fried prescribes, they would impose serious blocks to contracting. In the face of an unpredictable future, the requirement of equivalent performance would tend to discourage contract making. As a matter of fact, contracts function to lubricate cooperative arrangements because, under some circumstances, breach is encouraged by awarding damages that are less than would be awarded if equivalence were required. In many cases, allowing breach of contract may actually show more respect for autonomy by enabling individuals to respond reasonably to changing circumstances.

Freedom to breach is echoed in economic interpretations of contracting, such as the view proposed by R. Posner.[10] According to his view, a contract facilitates economic life by enforcing mutual expectations in a way that is designed to increase the economic welfare of the contractees. Against Fried's promise view, when economic welfare is not enhanced by a contract, *breach should be encouraged.* When, after paying damages, one person's gain through breach can override another's loss after paying damages, breach appears to make good economic sense. In fact, the notion of efficient breach has been incorporated as an interpretation of law in the *Restatement (Second) of Contracts.*

> The traditional goal of the law of contract remedies has not been compulsion of the promisor to perform his promise but compensation of the promisee for the loss resulting from breach. 'Willful' breaches have not been distinguished from other breaches, punitive damages have not been awarded for breach of contract, and specific performance has not been granted where compensation in damages is an adequate substitute for the injured party. In general, therefore, a party may find it advantageous to refuse to perform a contract if he will still have a net gain after he has fully compensated the injured party for the resulting loss.[11]

However, it is unclear in that work whether the breach is recommended for reasons of economic efficiency or out of an attempt to limit the coercive nature of contracts.[12]

In our view, the breach of a promise may be required by other moral considerations. Applying our view of promises to contracts, a court's demand for specific performance could be immoral, or, by requiring equivalent performance, as Fried desires, a court might unfairly punish one party to the reward of another. Our position is consistent with a court's rare demand for specific performance. Restitution for harm done by the promisor might be required, but specific or equivalent performance, in the face of seriously conflicting moral obligations, may not be justified.

However, we are not presenting a theory of contracts. Contracts are not promises, and we are not attempting to specify how courts should adjudicate contracts. Often, morality demands more than a court should or can enforce. Our point is that a contract, as a legal instrument, is not appropriately interpreted as a morally binding promise.

Therefore, although we believe that promising is immoral, we do not mean that contracting is immoral. On our view, if no promises were made, people could still engage in contracting. Yet when applied to contracts, our view about promises is more consistent with the actual behavior of courts than Fried's promise position. That is to say, contracts, like promises, cannot override other obligations.

Fried's theory suggests that all legitimate promises, those, for example, that are not coerced, should be legally enforced. This is not a standard interpretation of the law because, legally speaking, contracts must involve some "consideration," at least in most cases. This demand for consideration assumes that a contract is the outcome of a bargain: that something is given in exchange for performance. This is made clear in *Restatement (Second) of Contracts*:

> In the typical bargain, the consideration and the promise bear a reciprocal relation of motive or inducement: the consideration induces the making of the promise and the promise induces the furnishing of the consideration.[13]

While courts often do but sometimes do not require consideration, the fact that they often do suggests that a valid promise alone is not their only concern. In many cases courts demand at least the appearance of mutuality. This introduces a point of basic fairness which when absent can nullify a contract. Fairness is an element distinct from any obligation created by promising alone. Fried is unable to explain this requirement of mutuality; instead he points to "incoherence" in the legal use of consideration since it is sometimes demanded and sometimes not.[14] He concludes that in practice, the requirement of consideration is too inconsistent to challenge his doctrine. Unconvincingly, he claims that promisors always benefit from promises, getting at least the satisfaction of being able to realize their own purposes.[15] Once again, Fried seems to take an inflexible and ad hoc position on promises, and thus on contracts. Other values, like fairness, seem to play no role at all in his account.

Against Fried's view, courts have often based their judgements on reliance. This is at the heart of "promissory estoppel" used to provide compensation for damages stemming from partial performance before the finalization of a contract. A person may appeal to promissory estoppel to recoup loses when that person has reason to rely on the establishment of a bargain, even though a bargain is not consummated.[16]

Fried insists that a promise is fulfilled when the promisee receives what he or she expects. When this is not possible, as we have seen, Fried opts for the equivalent of what is expected. This is not a reliance principle, for while a person might expect certain gain after a promise is made, that person might not rely on the gain. In promissory estoppel, awards are not typically made on the basis of expectations but on losses caused by reliance. Against Fried's view, the *Restatement (Second) of Contracts* calls for remedy to be "limited as justice requires."[17] And Wellman points out, "recent courts . . . have been reluctant to award the full value of the promise when the reliance is considerably less."[18]

Reliance is not the only principle used by courts. In some cases they use a "restitution" principle. Suppose a person makes a deathbed promise to pay a million dollars for past services performed even though performed without demand for or agreement to pay. Suppose also that the services had a market value of $10,000. A court adjudicating a case like this in Wisconsin,[19] as explained by Vincent Wellman, gave the person involved an award that "was limited . . . to the reasonable value of the services she gave . . . plausibly a restitutionary measure."[20] Here the promise was judged to be unreasonable, though freely given and perhaps even relied upon. The content of the promise seemed to mean less to the court than fair compensation for services performed.

Most current theories about the nature and enforcement of contracts rely on principles and remedies not based on the simple willful creation of an obligation.[21] Some appeal to the customary purposes behind the creation of a contract as well as fairness, reliance, market value, or harm incurred. One such position, the relational contract theory, presented by Ian MacNeil,[22] thus moves away from the promise view. MacNeil insists that we cannot rely simply on the words of the contract but must also take into account background norms. Because all commerce occurs in a relational context, he argues that courts ought to take into account the norms implicit in a contract. As a matter of fact, contracts are regularly interpreted and informed in relation to laws such as the National Labor Relations Act. MacNeil's point is that background circumstances should, and often do, play such a role. On his interpretation contracts must be understood in a larger setting wherein they are subject to overriding and defining conditions that extend or limit the willed agreement of the parties.

Fried's view is individualistic in the sense that individuals are supposed to have the power and the right to bind themselves by promises and contracts. MacNeil's view, by contrast, appears to be more realistic in recognizing how contracts function in social life. Since contracts involve not only mutual agreement but also social norms and practices, adjudication on the basis of subjective intention alone is impractical. We need to keep in mind the fact that courts are third parties. They adjudicate contracts when there is a misunderstanding serious enough to lead the parties to seek adjudication. How courts proceed in such conflicts is crucial to understanding how obligations created by contracts are determined. The relational point of view underscores the role of background circumstances and so provides a basis for judging, in actual cases, whether the settlement of the contract is reasonable or fair.

Going further, Stewart Macaulay argues that contracts play but a small role in social life, including the life of business.[23] Working under the rubric "empirical contract theory," he claims, with plausibility, that people base their behavior on customary practices and the need for prompt and reliable performance more than on explicit contracts or promises. Disputes tend to be solved by appealing to general practices and business considerations. When people do resort to law, "statutory and administrative regulation, such as labor and corporate law, are more likely to affect behavior than the residual and therefore marginal law of contract."[24] His point is that the explicit creation of an obligation, even a legal obligation, plays little role in the day to day operation of commercial life. This consideration tends to diminish the claims of those who, like Hume, believe that without the ability to create specific moral obligations that assure future performance, business transactions, especially over time and distance, could not take place.

While the empirical view may understate the importance of contracts, it certainly seems to be true that an interpretation of contracts as promises, or as self-created obligations, is not needed to adjudicate contract disputes. Contracts are established and adjudicated against a background of needs, social practices, and laws. By contrast, Fried's view appears overly simplistic and impractical. Contrary to his belief, it also fails to provide additional security against breach. Our position is more in keeping with Hillman's account of contract law. In evaluating conflicting theoretical approaches, Hillman observes:

> Appropriating resources in an attempt to determine which set of principles 'wins' hardly seems worth the effort. In short, conflicting and complex theories, principles, rules, and policies dominate modern contract law and together govern the relations of people in our society.[25]

CONTRACTS AS ALTERNATIVES TO PROMISES

When taken seriously, a promise indicates a willingness to override other moral obligations. If not taken seriously by a promisor, a promise is deceptive in offering assurance. Assuming that we do, and must, rely on one another, are there means of prediction, other than promises, that can serve as bases of reliance? If so, are these alternatives similarly deceptive?

It is not difficult to find alternatives to promising that provide bases for reliance. Stanley Cavell points out that

> there are any number of ways, other than promising, for committing yourself to a course of action: the expression or declaration of an intention, the giving of an impression, not correcting someone's misapprehension . . . and so on.[26]

P. S. Atiyah observes that, in a sense, reliance itself may, at least in law, take the place of promises:

> [The] growing recognition among lawyers that one of the principal reasons for the enforcement of promises lies in the fact that they are, and are meant to be, relied upon, has led to an increased importance being attached to the fact of reliance itself. Justifiable reliance comes to be treated as in itself a sufficient ground for the imposition of an obligation; naturally then, it may in any particular case, be immaterial whether a statement is conceptualized as a promise or not.[27]

If Atiyah is correct, it is a mistake to think that promises are needed to create reliance, or a reasonable expectation of performance. First of all, we routinely suppose that, in many respects, the future will be like the past. When one sort of thing happens, another can be predicted to follow. Human actions can often be predicted because people act out of habit. We routinely rely on others to do what they are accustomed to do. Although such expectations may be disappointed, they are not necessarily less reliable than expectations based on promises, and they do not suffer from the problem of pretending to offer assurance.

We also rely, with some frequency, on people acting in their own self-interest. Employers believe that workers will do their jobs in order to receive their pay. An employer might reasonably rely more on performance based on pay than on performance based on a promise. Of course, if the employer pays low wages, or permits improper working conditions, he or she might prefer a promise. But this is exploitation; promises are, of course, sometimes used to exploit others. Such immoral reliance is not desirable and adds no support to the view that promises are morally desirable as a way to secure performance. In any case, genuine self-interest can be more effective than promises as a way of securing future behavior.

Let's assume that we have a simple arrangement based on pay. By a simple arrangement, we mean that before performance no apparent moral obligations are involved. If A works, A gets paid by B, but B is under no obligation to provide work for A even if A shows up. A can come or not as A wishes. B does rely on A to some degree, but B employs enough other workers to cover A's absence. Since B knows that enough workers show up on any given day to successfully carry on business, B's expectation is satisfied. Though no promise is made, both A and B have realistic expectations about the behavior of one another. A knows that work is typically available and B anticipates that an adequate number of workers will show up. These expectations are driven by mutual self-interest.

No promises are made; no new obligation is established. If A does not report to work, B is not deceived. It is likewise not deceptive if B has no work for A to do. A is free, morally speaking, to meet other moral requirements as they arise. There may be an agreement that specifies that A will receive from B a certain agreed upon wage for work completed. Such an agreement would not be a promise, however, because it is revocable. The agreement binds when the action is performed, but not otherwise. Although the parties to the agreement may have moral responsibilities in relation to justice and reliance, such responsibility is not created by promising.

Now suppose that A and B have drawn a contract. A agrees to work and B agrees to provide work for a specific number of hours per week under a set pay scale. By signing the contract, does A acquire a special moral obligation that would not have existed if there were no contract? We understand that a contract is intended to increase the likelihood of performance, and to clarify, as seems necessary, the terms of agreement. But is A morally bound by its terms?

In making the contract, B attempts to assure A's performance. Now if A does not perform, B has legal recourse. This is the point of the contract: to appeal to a practice, legal enforcement of contracts, to bring about the desired behavior. In this way contracts are similar to promises, for they are intended to provide assurance. But they differ from promises in several ways. Unlike promises, contracts are subject to independent adjudication. In the case of promises, the duty to perform, or the appropriateness of actions in case of breach, is subject to the interpretation of promisors and promisees. No promise can be complete in the sense that it covers all future contingencies, just as no contract can be complete. With promises, however, there is no procedure for settling disputes created by conflicting claims. Promisors and promisees act as both judges and jury. Unintentional bias on the part of the promisor or promisee is quite likely. Such bias can be a significant problem, especially when the consequences of keeping or breaking a promise are important to the parties involved.

Unlike a promise, a contract also does not guarantee performance. It does, however, subject the parties involved to the authority of independent adjudication. Even if one party believes that the terms of a contract have been satisfied to the letter, that person may end up in court. A judge may determine that the contract has been breached and damages should be awarded. Courts rarely require specific performance.

If A does not perform, A may be legally required to pay damages.

However, the court may find that the contract is not binding because, perhaps, it violates A's rights. The contract, in iteslf, does not create a moral obligation to perform. It is a legal instrument that subjects the parties involved to an independent and legally binding form of adjudication, whether such adjudication is wanted or not. If A breaches because, say, a better opportunity is found, then A may be willing to pay damages the court imposes. In such a case, the contract does the job it is intended to do by providing compensation for loss.

Of course, A may be morally bound to perform as contracted. By signing a contract, A is not excused from responsibilities determined by moral principles and rules. If B relies on A's performance, and A has no overriding moral obligations, then A may have a moral obligation to perform. But courts, it seems, are required to make legal judgments, not moral judgments, even if, in their deliberations, they may also be expected to take moral considerations into account. Indeed, in attempting to settle contract disputes, the courts usually become involved in cases of nonperformance, when contracts are being challenged or breached, whether or not such breach is morally justified. The focus of attention of the law in contract disputes is thereby different from the focus of private parties who make or receive promises. In promising, persons attempt to assure specific performance by the force of moral obligation but have no recourse to independent adjudication in case of default. In contracting there is less moral pressure on specific performance than upon the equitable settlement of disputes in cases of breach.

It is unreasonable to think that a contract, by itself, establishes a special moral obligation. A contract attempts to specify what is to be done and by whom, but, in the final analysis, liability is not necessarily dependent on the actual intentions of the contracting parties. Courts decide, in many different and sometimes conflicting ways, what a contract means. To be subject to such independent interpretation is what it means to make a contract: to place oneself under the coercive power of the courts. If a contract binds performance, it binds persons to the future and often unpredictable demands of the court. By the nature of contracting, persons cannot fully understand in advance what a contract will require them to do. They cannot be said to be morally bound, in advance, to perform according to the demands of the contract without fully knowing what those demands are.

A contract is a legal instrument which may lead to the imposition of the power of the state. Philosophers have explored the question of whether it is morally acceptable to use certain forms of state coercion in resolving contract disputes. One way to answer this question is by specifying necessary conditions for determining whether, morally speaking, a valid contract exists. If no valid contract exists, then one might argue that the state would be morally wrong to use its power of enforcement. For example, it might be claimed that contracts must be entered voluntarily and that the parties to the contract must be cognitively aware of its terms.

However, it is important to interject a distinction we made earlier about promises. This distinction applies to contracts as well, but it is often overlooked in the literature on contracts: the difference between the validity of a contract and the obligation not to breach. The point is that the conditions for a morally proper contract need not be the same as the conditions for moral a obligation to perform according to the conditions in the contract. For example, Michael J. Sandel seems to be unaware of this distinction in claiming that all contracts must be entered voluntarily and that they are also not valid if unfair.

> When two people make an agreement we may typically assess its justice from two points of view. We may ask about the conditions under which the agreement was made, whether the parties were free or coerced, or we may ask about the terms of the agreement, whether each party received a fair share.[28]

He goes on to say: "When I enter freely into an agreement, I am bound by its terms, whatever they may be," and that "contracts bind not because they are willingly incurred but because (or in so far as) they tend to produce results that are fair."[29] However, in talking about the validity of a contract, it is not accurate to claim that a valid contract entails being "bound by its terms." According to the judgments of courts persons are not necessarily bound by the terms of the contract. It is one thing to give an analysis of the validity of a contract, and quite another to analyze the conditions under which a person has a an obligation to *perform* as stipulated by the contract. In adjudication, this distinction is understood. Terms other than those mentioned in the contract are often used to adjudicate cases of breach. Courts may not require specific performance even when it is possible to do so. Indeed, the question of fairness is something the courts must decide. Although, certainly, the parties to a contract may try to follow existing statutes or, with legal assistance, predict what the ruling of a court might be, fairness cannot be assured or assumed at the time a contract is written.

Sandel's position seems to conflate the legal force of contracts and promises. Promises are usually supposed to create moral obligations, whereas contracts are thought to create legal obligations. These two forms of obligation are distinct. John Rawls accepts this distinction in his *A Theory of Justice*, claiming that obligations arising from institutions or practices do not by themselves create moral obligations. According to Rawls a duty to perform as contracted depends on moral principles, such as those he derives from the original position. Rawls observes that

> as citizens our legal duties and obligations are settled by what the law is, insofar as it can be ascertained. The norms applying to persons who are players in a game depend upon the rules of the game. Whether these requirements are connected with moral duties and obligations is a separate question.[30]

Although Rawls's view supports the distinction we are making between a legal and a moral obligation to perform, his position is not quite the same as ours. Whether a practice or institution has a moral force independent of moral rules or principles is a difficult issue, one we are not now addressing. We are examining whether a person has a moral obligation to perform an action based on past agreement. In the case of contracts, the answer is negative because legal practice does not typically require specific performance. Nevertheless, we do agree with Rawls, if this is what he means, that any moral obligation to perform depends upon what we ought to do "all things considered." We cannot forsake moral principles merely because we incur an institutional obligation, even if that obligation has a prima facie binding power.

In claiming that persons are not necessarily morally committed to perform according to the terms of a contract, we are not denying that standards may by used to judge the moral validity of a contract or that the courts cannot be morally correct or incorrect in enforcing a contract.

The mistake lies in thinking that the status of a contract determines the morality of keeping it, and this is a mistake that both Sandel and Fried seem to make. Part of the problem, as in the case of promises, is that the conditions at the time of making the contract may be different from conditions at the time the contract is scheduled to be kept. Another part of the problem is that the reasons offered to support the moral validity of contracts, for example, that they are in general socially needed, may be inconsistent with the enforcement of a particular contract, for example, because such enforcement would be socially harmful.

In the case of promising, the distinction we are making is more difficult to keep in mind because a promise is intended to give assurance of performance, where the assurance given is supposed to be known in advance, while a contract is understood as a legal document subject to subsequent legal interpretation that cannot be fully known or predicted. When we promise, we promise to perform; when we contract, we subject ourselves to the power of the courts.

Thus, contracts, unlike promises, provide some assurance without guarranteeing performance. A contract does not create a moral obligation to perform a specific deed. A contract is not a promise to do something but an agreement to either do it or else suffer the consequences of not doing it, as a court may decide. This is not to say that no one ever has an obligation to do the contracted thing. It means simply that contracts, unlike promises, are not decptive in assuring what cannot and hence should not be assured. Thus, in many ways, contracts are superior to promises. Contracts are subject to independent interpretation and enforcement. Contracts are usually more clearly formulated. For this reason contracts help prevent misunderstandings that often plague promises, including the kind of compensation that may be required when breach occurs. Contracts also involve some sort of mutuality, according to which both parties benefit, whereas the burdens and benefits of promises, on the other hand, are not equally shared. A contract typically stems from a desire for mutual gain and so tends to avoid exploitation. Although contracts may involve exploitation, the courts can sometimes compensate the exploited parties for injustice or harm.

As legal theorists have insisted, the enforcement of contacts must be balanced against other legal demands, including fairness. The enforce-

ment of contracts is bound up in a network of legal and social responsibilities and rights. To provide assurances, we have said that promises
must override other moral obligations. But the law recognizes that contracts are severely restricted by other legal requirements. In this way the
law realizes that contracts cannot bind categorically as promises are supposed to do, and hence avoids the most fundamental flaws inherent in
promising. Contracts do not negate the remainder of the law in the way
that promises, in order to be assurances, must negate the rest of morality.

NOTES

1. *Restatement of Contracts*, para. 1, 1932.

2. Charles Fried, *Contract as Promise: A Theory of Contractual Obligation*
(Cambridge: Harvard University Press, 1981).

3. G. Gilmore, *The Death of Contract* (Columbus, Ohio: Ohio State University Press, 1974), p. 88

4. Vincent A. Wellman, "Conception of the Common Law: Reflections
on a Theory of Contract," *University of Miami Law Review* 41 (1987): 934.

5. See Robert A. Hillman, "The Crisis in Modern Contract Theory," *Texas
Law Review* 67 (1988): 113–18 for a somewhat unfriendly account of the death
of contracts, claiming that contract law is flexible, yet does gives "ample guid-
ance to courts, lawyers, and parties." Hillman's point is eclectic. Contract law is
flexible, with a role for the actual bargain and a role for fairness as well.

6. Fried, *Contract as Promise*, p. 11.

7. Ibid., p. 17.

8. Ibid., p. 21.

9. Ibid., p. 38.

10. R. Posner, *Economic Analysis of Law* (Boston: Little, Brown, 1992).

11. *Restatement (Second) of Contracts* 1981, p. 100.

12. Jay M. Feinman, "The Significance of Contract Theory," *University of
Cincinnati Law Review* 58 (1990): 1298–99.

13. *Restatement (Second) of Contracts*, p. 173.

14. Fried, *Contract as Promise*, p. 35.

15. Ibid.

16. Hillman, "The Crisis in Modern Contract Theory," p. 115.

17. *Restatement (Second) of Contracts*, para. 90.

18. Vincent A. Wellman, "Conceptions of the Common Law," p. 962.

19. *In re* Gerke's Estate, 271 Wis. 297, 73 N.W.2d 506 (1955).

20. Vincent A. Wellman, "Conceptions of the Common Law," p. 969.

21. See Hillman, "The Crisis in Modern Contract Theory."

22. Ian Macneil, *The New Social Contract* (1980).

23. Stewart Macaulay, "An Empirical View of Contract," *Wisconsin Law Review* (1985): 465, and "Elegant Models, Empirical Pictures, and the Complexities of Contract," *Law and Society Review* 11 (1977): 507.

24. Feinman, "The Significance of Contract Theory," p. 1306.

25. Hillman, "The Crisis in Modern Contract Theory," p. 133.

26. Stanley Cavell, *The Claim of Reason: Wittgenstein, Skepticism, Morality, and Tragedy* (New York: Oxford University Press, 1979), p. 298.

27. P. S. Atiyah, "Promises and the Law of Contract," *Mind* 88 (1979): 416.

28. Michael J. Sandel, *Liberalism and the Limits of Justice* (New York: Cambridge University Press, 1982), p. 106.

29. Ibid., p. 107.

30. John Rawls, *A Theory of Justice* (Cambridge: Harvard University Press, 1971), p. 349.

seven

REASONABLE RELIANCE

It is not the oath that makes us believe the man, but the man the oath.
Aeschylus

We have been addressing two main questions: (1) whether making promises is morally justified, and (2) whether keeping promises is morally required. We have examined various conditions under which the making or keeping of promises may or may not be justified or required to underscore the point that such acts are not necessarily right or wrong. They are certainly not right or wrong just for being acts of those kinds. The rightness or wrongness of acts of any kind (except for acts defined in moral terms), including the making and keeping of promises, is determined by moral principles and rules. Even if one allows that the duty to keep promises is itself a moral rule, it must compete with moral principles and other moral rules in determining the justification of acts.

Indeed, we have emphasized the importance of separating questions about the justification or validity of making promises from questions about duties or obligations of promise keeping, because philosophers have often supposed, erroneously we believe, that questions about the obligating force of promises can be answered by answering questions concerning their justification or validity. The morally binding power of promises, we have maintained, is independent of their justification, and also independent of most of the supposed conditions of validity mentioned in the literature. The only condition of validity that seemed to withstand examination is that the person who makes a promise must do so intentionally. This condition, we have allowed, is a necessary condition for the existence of any duty or obligation of promise keeping. In response to the question of justification, our main point has been that, as a rule, the making of promises is morally wrong. However, we have not concluded that the duty to keep promises is therefore nullified, for this, we have said, is an independent issue.

The peculiarity of promising, as noted from the beginning, is that it supposes people can create obligations for themselves merely by proclaiming they have them: that they can nullify other duties by imposing a new obligation on themselves that overrides some, if not all, other moral considerations. This, we have argued, cannot be morally justified. People cannot be morally required to do what moral principles or rules prohibit them from doing. We have also maintained that making promises is unreasonable because no one can predict, much less control, all future contingencies. No one can reasonably assure anyone that he or she will make things happen the way they say they will.

In answer to the first question, then, we have claimed that making promises, generally speaking, is morally wrong because promises are made in order to assure what cannot reasonably be assured. There is a host of contingencies that may affect not only the morality of performing a promised act but its possibility as well. As a general rule, people should not make promises, because promises are deceptive and, in being deceptive, can create unreasonable reliance. We emphasize this point because the problem with promises is not simply that people do not always keep them, but that, as a rule, they should not make them in the first place. The problem with campaign promises is not always, as many seem to think, that politicians do not keep them, or sometimes should not keep them, but that their promises should not have been made, either because the thing promised would be wrong to do, or because the promisor was simply unrealistic, or a liar, in claiming to assure what cannot be assured. Politicians, it seems, would do better to keep their options open, in order to do what is right, instead of claiming they will stick to their guns.

But there may be exceptions to the rule. There may be times when making promises is justified. Subjectively, a person may make a promise in good conscience, *thinking* it is right and perhaps even required. Thus, according to some theories of responsibility at least, the person would not be subject to blame, even if, objectively speaking, the promise should not have been made. Making an unjustified promise in good faith does not differ from the performance of any other type of wrong act that an agent thinks is right.

Moreover, even from an objective point of view, there may be exceptions to the rule that persons should not make promises. There may be times when the need to give assurance is great, and hence that it would be good to make a promise, even if the promisor knew that the promise could not be kept, or that keeping it is unlikely. A promise may be justified even if the promisor has no intention of keeping it. In such a case, promising would be equivalent to telling a justified lie. Such lies may be categorized as useful fictions, or beneficent ones. One might argue that, if promises can be justified when there is no intention of keeping them, they certainly must be justified when there is an intention, and perhaps even a resolve, to do the promised thing. They certainly may be justified in such a case, but if a promise always assures more than can reasonably be assured, it always needs special justification.

Sometimes, indeed, promising is literally a game we play wherein we pretend the assurance is genuine, knowing full well it is not. We often know in our hearts that what we are pretending to guarantee cannot really be guaranteed (and those who receive the guarantee may know so as well), but we play the game nonetheless. When lovers promise one another that they will love each other always and forever, they are playing a kind of romantic game. Hypothetical desert island cases, where someone makes a promise to a dying person to do something trivial, like watering his plant until the promisor dies, seems to be of this kind. No one in his or her right mind would make such a promise, or expect it to be kept, except as a way of soothing the dying person by pretending to play along with an unreasonable wish. Assurances given to small children that Mom and Dad will never let anything harm them also seem to fall in this category: the creation of an illusory world wherein, it is believed, the lie will do little harm but, one hopes, a great deal of good. These kinds of promises are assurances about the future that immature people may really believe and rely on, or assurances that mature people *want* to believe, and even *pretend* are true, while, at the same time, they know are false. Promises are sometimes intended to give people hope, when the promisor, or even the promisee, knows there is little hope to give.

Many, naively, feel the same way about contracts. If they contract for something to be done, they expect it to be done, exactly as the contract says. But people with experience in business know that, for all sorts of reasons, contracts are broken, or are not completely satisfied, and that a contract, therefore, is no guarantee of performance. Contract law, which is institutionalized, in a way that promises are not, not only recognizes that contracts may be broken but, indeed, exists primarily to adjudicate cases where they are. However, making contracts is not, generally speaking, immoral, as making promises is, for just this reason: because contracts, unlike promises, are not guarantees. Just because we allow that contracts may be broken, for both good and bad reasons, we have provided for means of compensation according to the principles and precedents of law.

THE OBLIGATING FORCE OF PROMISES

In arguing that promising is immoral, we have set ourselves against those who uphold promising as an exemplary moral practice, a necessary element of organized society, or an essential feature of moral life. In opposition to these views, we have held that the so-called promising game is not only not necessary but also not a very good game to have or to play. Promising is wrong. This is what we believe that people in general, including philosophers, need to learn about promising. In order to avoid the harm that promises cause, people should be taught not to make promises. But, as a matter of fact, they often do make them. What, then, is required of them morally speaking? Our answer is that they should try to prevent the potential harm caused by their promises, if they can, and if there is no overriding moral obligation. The obvious and usual way of doing this is by keeping their promises.

Keeping a promise is usually the best thing one can do to prevent disappointed expectation or reliance, but the general duty of promise keeping does not redeem the practice of promising. Keeping a promise may prevent harm in a particular case, but even then its keeping could not have been assured. The prevention of harm in a particular case does not compensate for the possibility that, in that case and in many other cases, the keeping of the promise might be overridden by other considerations.

The harm caused by promise breaking is not limited to unjustified failures to keep promises but includes justified failures as well. People who justifiably fail to keep their promises disappoint expectation and reliance just as much as those who unjustifiably fail. One may raise questions of compensation in such cases, but that is a separate issue. There are no generally accepted procedures governing compensation for broken promises, which is one of the reasons why such procedures have been created in law to compensate persons harmed by breach.

Therefore, it is just because promises can and often do create expectation and reliance that there is a prima facie case for claiming that promises ought to be honored. We say a "prima facie" case because there is no *necessary* connection between the making of a promise and the duty to keep it. We have argued that there is no necessary connection between a justified promise and a duty to keep it, or between an unjustified promise and a duty not to keep it. The reason for this is that the expectation or reliance created by a promise, whether or not justified, may or may not tip the balance of obligations in favor of keeping the promise according to moral principles and rules.

Since the prima facie rule bidding persons to keep promises can conflict with other moral rules and principles, it does not always determine a particular obligation or, in the language of Ross, an actual duty. Indeed, we believe that the promise-keeping rule is itself derived from higher principles, such as benevolence, nonmaleficence, and justice, and is in fact subordinate to an even more general rule, also so derived, that persons ought to do what they have assured or intentionally led others to expect they will do. One might call this the intentionally created reliance rule. Thomas Scanlon has tried to formulate such a rule in his "Promises and Practices," where he argues that the duty of promise keeping does not require a social practice to support it, for, on his view, it is derivable from a more general principle.[1] After warning that "one must exercise due care not to lead others to form reasonable but false expectations," he adds that "if one has created such expectation, then one must take reasonable steps to prevent that loss." "My aim," he says, "is to defend a general principle of fidelity that can account for obligations arising from promises and other instances of explicit and intentional expectation."

Such a principle or rule may be supposed to support not only promise keeping but also, for example, contracts and agreements as well. It may even be said to apply to duties attached to a person's station in life, as firefighters are expected to put out fires, and physicians are expected to treat patients, because, by taking these jobs, they have intentionally led others to believe that they can be counted on to do such things. This more general principle or rule also expresses a prima facie duty, of course, and hence does not, independently of other considerations, determine an actual duty, or a particular obligation, all things considered. It may turn out that the thing relied upon is not a good for the person who relies upon it, or it may be harmful for others. The prima facie rule that bids us to satisfy reliance, which is supported by the beneficence and nonmaleficence principles, may also be overridden by those principles in particular cases.

The importance of reliance in determining the duty of promise keeping is tied to the beneficence and nonmaleficence principles because good may be accomplished if the relied upon action is performed or harm may be caused if the relied upon action is not performed. Indeed, reliance itself may impose a duty on someone even if that person did nothing to create the reliance. A person may have a duty to help another who relies on him or her for help, even if the person who has this duty did not intentionally or otherwise lead the other person to expect such assistance. But, in the case of promises, contracts, and agreements, such reliance is intentionally created, and hence imposes a special obligation on the person who creates it. This special obligation does not follow from the benevolence and nonmaleficence principles alone but from these in conjunction with a principle of justice. Pall S. Ardal writes:

> Since the promisor raises the expectations in the promisee by the promise, and in most cases intentionally does this, he is responsible if he failed to do what he has promised to do. The evil or deprivation coming to the promisee is due to the promisor. He ought therefore not to break his promise.[2]

Justice comes into play because the promisor or contractor is responsible for creating the reliance. The duty falls to the promisor, not simply because he or she is the one relied upon, but because he or she created the reliance. The harm done by any failure to satisfy the expectation is harm caused by that person's intentional action. Others may acquire duties if a promisor promises that *they* can be relied upon, or if a promisor fails to keep a promise and others find themselves in a position to prevent the harm caused by such failure, but theirs would not be a duty of promise keeping. It may be a duty of charity if, indeed, a duty at all. Reliance, however, is a necessary condition of any actual duty or obligation of promise keeping. If there were no reliance, there would be no duty.

Thus, an actual duty to perform a promised act requires as necessary conditions that (1) the promise is intentionally made, and (2) there is reliance on performance. An actual duty to perform also requires, of course, that (3) performance of the promised act is possible, and (4) there is no overriding duty to perform another act or to refrain from performing the promised act. We do not hold that the mere possibility, or even the probability, of doing more good than would be done by keeping the promise is necessarily an overriding consideration, although, in some cases, a duty of charity may indeed override a duty of promise keeping. The statement of these necessary conditions seems to bring us very close to a statement of sufficient conditions.

There has been some debate over whether expectation or reliance determines the obligation of promise keeping. Some authors appear to believe that it is one and not the other, and still others, like Scanlon, hold that it is both. In his article, "The Value of a Promise," Dennis M.

Patterson challenges Scanlon's claim that the binding power of promises depends on both expectation and reliance, arguing that these criteria are separate and incommensurable. They are separate, Patterson maintains, because expectation is based on intention and reliance on actions.

> The basic problem with putting reliance and expectation together in a single theory of promising is that the conceptual nerve of each interest or principle consistently undermines the other. At war are two independent grounds of obligation: is it what a person expects (intention) that makes a promise binding or is it what he does (action) in reaction to the making of promise? The basic distinction here is between intention and action.[3]

But surely expectation and reliance are not exclusive. A promisee may both expect performance and rely on it. Indeed, persons normally rely on promises *because* they expect them to be kept. It is not entirely clear what Patterson means by saying that expectation involves intention and that reliance involves action, except that expectation is a mental state and reliance is often expressed in action (or by foregoing action). Nevertheless, actions are also intentional, and expectation itself is a kind of reliance. A promisee who expects an action to be performed, and wants it to happen, does have an emotional investment in its performance, and hence relies, even if the promisee takes no action predicated on such performance. In any case, our point, and apparently Scanlon's also, is that the disappointment of expectation and/or reliance are types of *harms;* the very types of harms most obviously associated with failures to keep promises. In characterizing promises as assurances, Scanlon sees that the harm caused by breaking promises is the harm caused by giving assurances and failing to make good on them. To say that that harm takes the form of disappointed expectation or reliance means that *the harm is caused by dependence on the assurance.* To say that a promisee, and perhaps others as well, expect or rely on the fulfillment of a promise is to say that they have come to depend on it for some good.

Pall S. Ardal appears to agree on the point that the obligation of promise keeping can be explained only in terms of good produced or evil avoided, but he also seems to believe that the weight of this point cannot be supported by the concept of reliance alone. Reliance, he says, is a sufficient but not a necessary condition for an obligation of promise keeping, because there can be an obligation of prormise keeping in cases where there is no reliance. Arguing against Neil Mac-Cormick, who holds a reliance theroy of obligation, Ardal writes:

> MacCormick's explication of reliance in terms of preparedness to make plans or take action has to be rejected if he is attempting to provide necessary conditons for successful promising. Many promises are made that in no way affect possible plans or action of the promisee. . . . Although he has thus given sufficient conditions for the making of a promise, these conditons are, as we have seen, by no means necessary.[4]

Although Ardal's language shifts improperly from talk of conditions necessary for obligations of promise keeping to conditions necessary for promise making, his claim is that there can be obligations to keep promises in cases where there is no reliance. But, even if so, reliance is not a sufficient condition for obligation, for, obviously, someone may rely on the keeping of a promise that it would be wrong to keep. Reliance is not even a sufficient condition for making a promise, for a person may rely when no promise is made.

To make his point that reliance is not necessary for an obligation of promise keeping, Ardal focuses attention on promises to the dead or dying and on threats, holding that dead persons cannot rely on the keeping of a promise and that persons who are threatened with harm cannot be said to rely upon receiving that harm.

> The most spectacular cases not covered are death-bed promises. . . . What are the dying person's future plans or actions?
>
> It should be noted that it is often obligatory to carry out one's threats: they may be beneficial to the person threatened as well as to others. But if the threatened person does not see the benefit the whole of the obligation could hardly derive from the fact that the promisee has been relying on the threat to be carried out. He may on the contrary be hoping that that will not.[5]

Ardal appears to believe that there can be obligations to keep promises to the dead and that there can be duties to carry out threats, because of the good produced for the promisee or the person threatened. Thus, on his view, it need not be reliance of the promisee that creates the obligation (or of anyone else for that matter) but some good they receive from keeping the promise.

But surely the duty to keep a promise must be dependent upon the promise; otherwise one might have a duty to do what is promised but not *because it was promised*. The mere making of a promise, or the giving of assurance, we have argued, does not alone create an obligation of promise keeping, nor does the mere doing of some good, even if assured. There needs to be a *connection* between the good to be done and the assurance such that the need for doing the good is created by the assurance. The concept of reliance is used to bring out the idea that there must be dependence. Now, Ardal may be right in thinking that "reliance," as used by MacCormack, is too narrow a concept to account for all cases of dependence, for MacCormack appears to think of reliance in terms of action based on assurance, as Patterson does. Undoubtedly, reliance is often expressed in action, but it can also be expressed by expectation without action, and there is even a broader sense of reliance in which it simply means dependence, even when there is no expectation, action, or even awareness of such dependence. Perhaps this is what Ardal has in mind when he speaks of obligations of promise keeping based on benefits to persons other than the promisee, for they may depend on the keeping of a promise even if they do not consciously or actively rely.

In our previous example of the car salesperson who promises delivery of a car, knowing full well that delivery cannot be guaranteed, we said that the promise was not justified. But we also pointed out that there may be an obligation to keep the promise nonetheless. The customer may have relied on the promise, not only by expecting delivery, but also by planning accordingly. If the car was promised for Friday, the customer may have made plans for the weekend, preparing a trip by car and making hotel reservations and appointments with friends in another city. They, in turn, may have made preparations for the visit, buying additional groceries, canceling other plans, and so on. There are *consequences* created by reliance on a promise which would not have been created if no promise were made. It was wrong for the salesperson to mislead the customer at the time of making the promise, but it would also be wrong for the salesperson not to keep the promise, if it turns out to be possible to do so, all things being equal. The duty to keep this promise could be overridden by other considerations, of course, but there does seem to be a strong prima facie reason for keeping it. The promise altered the behavior of the customer who relied on it. It also altered the behavior of others who, in turn, planned their lives accordingly. Failure to keep the promise deprives them of good they depend on *because of the promise.*

There are also cases in which persons other than the promisee not only depend on the keeping of a promise but are also its intended beneficiaries. Thus, instead of analyzing promises solely in terms of a promisor's promising something to a promisee, the analysis can be expanded to include a promisor's promising an action to a promisee for the sake of one or more third parties. Jones promises Smith that she will help Doe. Smith is assured that Doe's benefit will be provided by Jones. Smith relies on Doe's receiving this benefit from Jones. The harm that comes from any failure to keep the promise is, therefore, primarily a harm to Doe, although it may also harm Smith who has an interest in Doe's welfare. Doe relies on Jones for this benefit even if Doe doe not know about Jones' promise and does not consciously expect the benefit. But Smith consciously relies, for Smith foregoes other options that might have been chosen to insure the welfare of Doe.

At least some cases of promises to the dead may be construed in this way. They are analogous to the making and execution of a will wherein the executor is expected to carry out the intentions or dictates of a person who has died. Although there may be no promise in such a case, a person who makes a will relies on the executor to provide for others. The executor may thus be said to have an obligation to the person who dies, but the beneficiaries are living persons. If we suppose that, in addition to or in lieu of a will, the dying person gives power of attorney to another, because the other promised to carry out his or her wishes, there might then be a duty of promise keeping. It would be a promise to a dying person to help someone else.

The beneficiary of a promise might in fact be the promisor. A parent may elicit a promise from a child to look both ways before crossing the street. Although, obviously, the parent may profit from the keeping of the promise, and even depend on it, the child's welfare is the direct object of the parent's concern. If this were a deathbed promise, the child would profit but not the parent. The parent receives the value of being assured, but that is a function of making the promise, not of keeping it. However, in considering such cases, we should be careful to note again that the good produced by keeping the promise, or the evil avoided, may not be dependent on the promise. Looking both ways before crossing may help insure the child's safety, but that would be true even if there were no promise. The promise in this case does not create a state of affairs that would not have existed if no promise were made.

David B. Seligman makes this point about threats. In his article "A Threat or a Promise," he observes that promises are generally assurances of some good, or of something that the promisee wants, whereas threats are assurances of some harm, or something the person threatened does not want.[6] He allows, as Ardal does, that persons sometimes have a duty to carry out threats, but he also points out that such duties are not usually created by the threat. A parent may threaten a child with discipline and have a duty to carry out the threat, because such discipline is necessary, but not because it is threatened. A threat may justifiably be carried out, to make good on the threat, just as a promise may be carried out to make good on the promise, to accomplish the good that the threat is intended to accomplish. But such good may not be dependent on the threat. People *might* depend on the carrying out of threats, as citizens might depend on the threat of law enforcement against criminals. In such cases threats may be construed as promises, and there may be a duty to carry them out. The persons threatened would not be the beneficiaries of the threat, unless one supposed that law enforcement is for their benefit as well.

One of the problems we must face in attempting to test our theory, or any theory, by the use of examples and counterexamples, is that there is apt to be a difference of opinion about whether, in the examples being considered, an obligation of promise keeping does or does not exist. As Paul Ziff remarks, rather humorously, in his *Epistemic Analysis*:

> If you fail to perform a promise to meet with me for a drink, and your excuse is that you had to care for an injured rabbit in your garden, would that excuse serve to exonerate you form all blame? It would

with me. It would not with some others, who can remain unmention-able. What if your excuse were that you had to care for a displaced har-vestman, a splendid Daddy-Long-Legs? Again, that would be an acceptable excuse to me, but, I am sure, not to many others.[7]

And if such disagreement is common, even in apparently normal cases, we should expect even less agreement about unusual or abnormal cases, such as desert-island examples where the existence of an obligation is dubious and contentious. One is likely to beg the question in such cases in favor of the theory one is trying to defend. But such difference of opinion about the binding force of promises is one of the reasons we have offered for claiming that promising is itself morally wrong. Promises are deceptive and capable of causing harm just because they can create unreasonable expectation or reliance. The duty to keep promises, by and large, just is the duty to prevent that harm. Since the whole point of promising is to give assurance, over and above any other obligation a person may have, it seems that there could be no basis for a duty of promise keeping other than reliance on that assurance. That certainly seems to be the explanation of why, normally, there is no obligation when the promisee releases the promisor from the promise.

THE RIGHTS AND DUTIES OF PROMISEES

That is also why we argued earlier that persons who take their own promises seriously, and who are, in this sense, more reliable promisors, are likely to have a greater obligation to keep their promises, because other people are likely to rely on them more. Likewise, promises made to naive promisees are likely to create greater reliance and a stronger prima facie duty. Perhaps no one should be taken in by the promises of salespersons, but, of course, many are, and their reliance thus creates a prima facie obligation.

As W. D. Woozley points out, it is important to distinguish the guar-anteeing function of promises from their obligating function.[8] People tend to rely on promises because promises are guarantees, or are taken to be guarantees, and the reliance creates the obligation to perform, if and when there is an obligation. The obligation, in turn, may be said to create a correlative right to performance. That is, any right of the promisee to performance follows upon the promisee's reliance. The reliance cannot be founded on any predetermined right. If there were no reliance, there would be no obligation, and hence no right.

Now, a promisee who receives a promise may *think* that he or she has a right to performance, just because the promise is made, but he or she can be said to have a prima facie right at best. The reliance may be a result of the promisee's thinking that there is a right to performance, but he or she may have no actual right, if indeed the promisor has no corresponding actual obligation. A promisor who promises something that it would be wrong to do would have no obligation to do it even if the promisee wanted it done. But the promisee may rely nonetheless, *because it was promised*, taking the promisor at his or her word. The reliance is not predicated on the *right* to rely but on the promise or *guarantee* of performance. Thus, the right does not create the reliance; the reliance creates the right.

The question of whether the promisor has an actual obligation to do the promised act depends on, among other things, the reliance of the promisee. The promisor may or may not know fully the extent of such reliance but must make his or her judgment on the basis of available information. If, however, the promisee relieves the promisor of obligation, by indicating there is no reliance, the promisor is off the hook, unless, of course, others also rely. The promisee, in turn, is in a better position to know the extent of his or her reliance, but the promisee may not know the promisor's other duties as well as the promisor does. Thus, there is ample room for disagreement over the existence of an actual duty on the part of the promisor, or an actual right on the part of the promisee.

It seems more appropriate to speak of reasonable or unreasonable expectation of performance rather than a right to rely. The expectation follows upon the assurance: it is a function of the belief of the promisee that the promise will be kept. It is not a function of the right to believe, or the right to expect performance. Even if one did have a right to expect performance, there may be good reason not to expect it, and there may be reason to expect it, even if there is no right. Reasonable people, we have argued, do not expect performance simply because it is promised but because they think they have good reason to rely on the person who makes the promise.

One might argue that, if it is unreasonable, and hence wrong, to make promises, it is also unreasonable, and hence wrong, to rely on them. However, the assurance given by a promise, if taken at face value, is absolute, and, for this reason, unrealistic, whereas the promisee's reliance on a promise need not be. Promises themselves are sometimes viewed as conditional, or as conditioned by background assumptions, but if promises are looked at in this way, they are not genuine assurances. The point of promising is to guarantee performance, and this is why the assurance given by promises is deceptive. If taken at face value, promises may be relied upon unduly. But a promisee's reliance need not be absolute. Reliance can vary in extent or degree. Even though promises are offered as guarantees of performance, reasonable people will allow for the possibility, and even the very real probability, that the promise will not be kept. They will allow that the person who makes the promise may not be able to keep it, or that keeping a promise may conflict with some other duty the promisor has, or even that a given promisor may be insincere or otherwise unreliable. Thus, on the side of the promisee, there are contingencies and background conditions to consider: the very sorts of contingencies that make promising immoral. For this reason, a person who relies too heavily on a promise may also be at fault for expecting more than he or she should reasonably expect.

In our example of the car salesperson, we should note that the salsperson made a promise to the car buyers but not anyone else. Others may depend on the keeping of the promise but neither they nor the salesperson may know about such dependence. Thus, we cannot expect the salesperson to take their specific dependence into account unless told by the buyers that they and others depend. The others, in fact, are dependent on expectations created by the buyer (whether or not created by another promise) and not simply on the promise of the salesperson. The buyers created this expectation on the basis of the salesperson's promise, but they, in turn, may also bear responsibility for intentionally creating expectation of or reliance upon something they could not reasonably assure. Others who thus made plans accordingly, if reasonable, should also have known that the car buyers might not arrive as planned.

Thus, the harm of disappointed expectation or reliance in this case is caused, if it is, not only by the car salesperson who fails to deliver the car, but also by the car buyers who fail to keep their appointments with friends, and by the friends who may have relied unduly on such expectation. After all, they have no more right to rely upon an unreasonable assurance than others have a right to give one.

The reasonableness of reliance is based, not on moral considerations, or on what, ideally, people ought to do, but on natural, nonmoral considerations, such as simple induction from past experience. Generally speaking, it is reasonable to rely on people who have been reliable in the past, and it is unreasonable to rely on people who have not been reliable in the past. There may be exceptions, as in emergency situations, when we may be forced to rely on persons we would not otherwise rely upon, simply because we have no choice. One might, for example, rely on a drunken driver to take one to the hospital in a medical emergency if no other form of transportation were available. But we have argued that normally it would not be reasonable for promisees to rely upon unreliable promisors. Indeed, it may be said that promisees have no right to rely on the promises of unreliable promisors, if they know or have good reason to believe that they are unreliable. Such reliance is irresponsible because it is unrealistic, and it may be harmful if unreliable promisors are relied upon to perform important tasks. Under normal conditions, it would be wrong to entrust one's children to a previously unreliable baby-sitter even if that person promised to change. Thus, promisees may be at fault for relying on promisors just as promisors may be at fault for creating false expectations. The fault of promise making, and hence unreasonable reliance, is in fact encouraged by people who insist that others promise things they cannot or will not deliver. The unreasonableness of the expectation, however, does not relieve the baby-sitter of the obligation to perform, for it was the intention of the baby-sitter to create that expectation.

Some of the paradoxes we have cited are based on simple induction from past experience. An immoral promisor, who is immoral not only for making promises, but for trying to keep them, no matter what, is a more reliable promisor than a person who rightly tries to avoid making promises, or when making them, allows that they may be overridden by other moral considerations. But because immoral promisors are likely to create reliance, they are more likely to create an obligation to perform. Likewise, in societies where persons take promising very seriously, the duty to keep promises is likely to carry more weight, just because promises are relied upon more. In a society where promises are not taken very seriously, people are not as likely to rely on them. Since reasonable people at least would not rely, there would be no reliance or expectation to disappoint.

The upshot of these remarks, if we are correct, is that the assurance given by a promise, or reasonable reliance upon performance, is not determined by the obligating force of promises, or by any so-called right to rely. *The assurance or reliance function of promises does not depend on their ability to create obligations.* This point appears to need emphasis because nearly all philosophers seem to think that reasonable reliance on promises is backed by their obligation-creating force. If we are correct, the fact that promises do or do not create obligations is irrelevant. When it comes to reliance, what we need to know is whether the promisor is or is not likely to do what he or she says, and *that* is independent of whether or not he or she has an obligation to do it. After all, people may be counted on to do what they promise, even if what they promise is morally wrong.

Rejecting the view that "in promising one is putting oneself under an obligation and that this is the whole point of pormising," Ardal illustrates his point by the following example:

> A boy-friend makes a girl promise to sneak out after her mother and father are asleep. He may request the promise because he thinks that she ought not to do this. . . . In this case she could well say 'I promise you, although I know I ought not to do what I promise you.' What one cannot say is 'I promise you, but I don't intend to do what I promise you to do.'[9]

In such a case, it may be reasonable to rely even though there is no right to rely. Threats are a good example. Threats are sometimes excluded from the class of acts called promises because threats are not wanted by the person threatened, or are not good for that person. It would be more accurate to say, on our view, that threats *are* promises but that there is no prima facie obligation to keep them: they are assurances, even if what they assure is wrong. Suppose that the person threatened knows that the person who makes the threat has a reputation for keeping his or her word: that is what makes the threat effective. The person threatened, afraid that the threat will be carried out, takes steps to avoid the harm. This action would not be taken because the person threatened has a right to expect performance. There is no right to expect performance because there is no obligation to perform, but the person threatened has good reason to expect performance nonetheless. This is a reasonable expectation even though there is no right on the part of the promisee and no obligation on the part of the promisor. Carrying out a threat *might* be justified, even required, even if not wanted by the person threatened, for there might be other overriding considerations. A threat might be justified, and even required, because it is relied upon, even if not wanted in and of itself. P. S. Atiyah points out that, in contract law, reliance on a threat can create a legal obligation, for, in view of a threat, a person may have arranged his or her life accordingly.[10]

Vows may also be thought to be different from promises, but for different reasons. It is, of course, possible to vow to do something wrong, harmful, or not wanted, in which case a vow may also be a threat. But, obviously, vows may also be made to do things that are considered good, such as vows exchanged in a marriage ceremony. Vows are promises, it appears, except that they appear to be especially strong promises because they call upon a higher authority, such as God. The belief that vows are more binding than promises may, of course, create greater expectation or reliance, and hence create a greater obligation or duty, all things equal. But, morally speaking, it is the seriousness of the consequences of breaking such vows that makes them more binding, when and if they are. Divorce, for instance, can cause serious emotional and economic harm. But it does not always do so, and even when it does, it may be the lesser of evils. When people stay married, they may do so because they have promised, or because they have taken a vow, but the only good reason for doing so, in our view, is because staying married is better than other alternatives, all things considered. Such benefit is dependent on reliance, of course: reliance that would not have existed if no vows were taken.

A belief in God, or some higher power, may alter the picture, because one may suppose that, in the case of a vow, there are external sanctions for breaking or keeping it that are absent in the case of promises. In this respect, vows may begin to look more like contracts, as, indeed, marriage is considered to be a contract. Sanctions, imposed by God, or by law, can alter the consequences of keeping or failing to keep a vow, and hence affect the obligation to keep it. But the principle remains the same. Vows, like promises, are binding or not binding, morally speaking, accordingly as it is right or wrong to perform the act according to moral principles and rules. The taking of a vow does not bind categorically any more than a promise does.

What, then, is the force of saying, "You promised, you said you would"? Is so-saying a good reason for holding someone responsible? On our account, it *can* be a reason, but it is only a prima facie reason, not a sufficient one. The point of saying, "You promised" is to remind the promisor of his or her assurance, but any claim against the promisor needs to be backed by an appeal to reliance: "I waited for you for an hour and you failed to come." "I counted on you because you said you would." If there was a promise but no reliance, the promisor could respond, "Yes, I said I would, but I learned in advance that you would not be there." The absence of reliance, we argued earlier, does not nullify a promise by making it an invalid promise, but it does nullify the obligation to perform. At least it nullifies the obligation to perform *because* the action was promised, although there may be an obligation to perform for some other reason.

It appears to be a mistake to believe that promises can create obligations only for promisors or, for that matter, that they can create rights only for promisees. In the above example, the person who accepts the promise of a meeting also seems to take on a prima facie obligation to attend: the promisor's obligation is contingent on the promisee's holding up his or her end of the deal. Otherwise there would be no reliance, and hence no obligation. But suppose the promisee sends someone else to the meeting and the promisor fails to attend? In such a case, it seems, the promisee does rely. The promisee responded to the assurance by making plans accordingly. But the terms of the assurance were different. The promisor promised to meet the promisee, not someone else.

Other variations are possible. In a marriage ceremony, a bride and groom may vow to love and support one another until death. They soon have children, but the children were not mentioned in the original deal. Do they have an obligation to the children? Well, it seems, they obviously do. But does this obligation follow from the marriage vows? Well, in a sense, the answer again is "Yes." The welfare of the children depends on keeping the marriage vows even though the children were not mentioned in them. The children do rely, although they personally were not led to rely—at least they were not led to do so by the vows. Nonetheless, the reliance of the children affects the morality of keeping the vows. In this type of case, we may suppose the parties involved *know* of the reliance. In the case of the meeting, where the promisee sends someone else, the promisor may not know this. So the promisor may cause harm, because of reliance, but not be responsible for doing so. At least the promisor would not be responsible if the promisor believed the promisee would not attend and had no reason to think anyone else would. Communication about such a change in plans may or may not be possible, but the promisee would seem to have a prima facie duty to inform the promisor of such change if it were possible to do so. The promisor might then have the right to withdraw the promise.

Suppose the promisor thinks the promisee will attend the meeting, but the promisee does not attend. The promisor thus assumes there is reliance when there is none. Well, again, subjectively, the promisor would be under a prima facie obligation to show up for the meeting, although, objectively, no harm would be done to the promisee by failing to keep the promise. But harm is done to the promisor, and the promisee would be at fault for not attending, all things being equal.

As we have said, the good or evil caused by keeping or failing to keep a promise is not limited to the promisee, for, as in the case of the children mentioned above, others may be affected as well. Likewise, the good or evil caused by the commission or omission of a promised act may or may not depend on the action or inaction of the promisor. One might say, "*You* should do it because *you* promised you would," but as much good, and even more good, may be accomplished if someone else does it instead. It can matter whether the promised act is done by the promisor, of course. If a rock star promises to give a concert, it matters whether or not that star appears. The obligation is not satisfied by sending someone else instead. The children may *want* Mom to take them to the circus on Saturday, not Dad. But, often, what matters is that the thing is done, and not by whom. Sometimes, indeed, one promises that another will do something, in which case it may be important that the promisor *not* do it.

There is then a question of whether promises make any difference at all. Our answer has been, yes, but only if a promise creates reliance that would have been absent if there were no promise. Yet promises are not the only way of creating reliance, so the question is whether promises create any greater obligation or duty. Moreover, is there any good reason to rely on promises more than on other ways of predicting future behavior? These questions are not the same, we have said, for a promisor may have a duty to keep a promise even if the promisee has no good reason to expect performance, and there may be good reason to expect performance even if there is no duty to perform. It seems important to reiterate this point, since many philosophers seem to believe that our ability to rely on the future actions of others depends on the duty-creating force of promises. It does not, we have argued, because there are other, and sometimes even better, ways of predicting future behavior, whereas promises themselves are, in fact, no guarantee at all. Thus, the question, "Do these other ways create obligations in the same way promises do?" is distinguishable from the question, "Can we rely on these other ways of predicting the future as much as we can rely on promises?" The answer to the latter question is obviously "Yes." The answer to the former question is more complicated but, in a sense, moot. It is moot when it comes to predicting the actions of others, which is the *only* thing we need to know when planning or deliberating about our own actions. That is, if we are reasonable, we do not plan our own lives on the basis of what we think others *should* do but on the basis of what we believe they *will* do. We may, of course, encourage others to do what we think they should, or even hold them responsible for their failures, and these are ways of trying to *change* their behavior— by the force of moral suasion, by censure, or by punishment and reward. The question about whether promises create obligations, then, from the standpoint of promisees, is really a question about whether we should, as a rule, encourage or not encourage people to keep their promises. But we can also hold people responsible for creating reliance in other ways.

Persons can create expectations by contracts or agreements, by expressions of intention, or by simply telling others what they plan to do. The real difference between promises and other expectation-creating acts, we have said, is that promises give assurances, whereas the other acts do not. But this is also precisely what we have claimed is *wrong* with promises. The very thing that makes them different is not a virtue but a fault. The fault of promises is that they give *false* assurances by creating the impression that promised acts are being guaranteed when, in fact, there can be no such guarantee.

Suppose the matter is serious and the consequences great. Someone asks two friends to keep a secret, knowledge of which, if revealed to others, would ruin the person's reputation, and perhaps even cause a loss of employment or a breakup of the family. The one friend says, "I promise I will never tell." The other, however, has reservations, saying, "I really can't promise, but you know that I'm a good friend and that I would never tell, except under the most unusual circumstances." The person who makes the request may feel more assured by the first response than by the second but seems to have little choice but to rely on both, or else start thinking about what to do if the secret is revealed. Indeed, the person with the secret should probably give serious thought to this possibility in any case, for even the friend who makes the promise may not keep it, or the secret may be revealed in some other way. In any case, let us suppose that, sometime later, a situation arises in which revealing the secret can save a life or prevent an innocent person from being falsely accused. The question is: Does the person who promised have an obligation that is more binding than that of the person who did not promise? The answer seems to be, all things being equal, no. Of course, if one person tells, or the secret is revealed in some other way, there may be no need for one or the other to provide the information, although, even then, there may be need for corroboration. In this case, it is important to notice that it is not only the expectation or reliance that tips the balance in favor of keeping or breaking the promise but the seriousness of the matters involved. It seems that the promisee has no choice but to rely on the friend who did not promise as much as the friend who did. The promise does not place on the promisor any greater moral obligation than the promisor would have had if there were no promise.

Would it have been reasonable for the promisee to rely more on the person who promised than on the person who did not promise? Not necessarily. If the promisor were the kind of person who tends to keep promises, no matter what, and if the promisee knows this, then the promisee would have good reason to rely. But, in this case, the promisee would then be relying on the promisor to do something immoral. If the promisor were a moral promisor, then he or she would not keep the promise, no matter what. Indeed, according to our analysis, if that person were moral, the promise would not have been made in the first place. In any case, the promise adds nothing to reasonable expectation or reliance, the very thing promises are supposed to do.

Some people, such as priests, lawyers, psychotherapists, and journalists, are supposed to keep secrets or confidences if revealed to them under certain specified conditions, as duties of their offices. They need not make explicit promises to each and every client, for clients assume that their secrets will be kept as a matter of duty. But, of course, even then, clients should realize that professionals are fallible and do not always do their duty. Professionals may also be torn between the demands of conflicting duties and hence, as a matter of conscience, choose to violate a confidence. Suppose the situation is similar to the one described above. A secret is told to a professional who is bound to secrecy; the matter is serious, and yet even greater harm or injustice can be avoided if the secret is told. Would the professional be obligated or even permitted to betray the confidence?

This type of case differs from the former in various ways. In the first place, it is probably the case that the professional involved did not know the secret beforehand but was told only on the assumption that it would not be revealed. A second difference is that the professional is supposed to be bound by the duties of office and is, indeed, functioning in an institutional role specifically designed to inspire trust. For these reasons, there seems to be an even greater obligation than there would be in the case of a simple promise not backed by institutional support. If so, promising is not only not the only way of creating reliance, or an obligation to perform—it is not even the best way.

Now, one may suppose, legal considerations aside, that a priest, or a lawyer, or a therapist, has an absolute moral duty not to betray a confidence under any circumstances. However, in considering assurances backed by institutions, we have raised the questions: are the institutions themselves justified, and, if so, are persons in such institutional roles always bound to do what the rules of their roles in life dictate they should? Is such expectation reasonable, given other duties and obligations? Our answer has been that it makes sense for such people to try their best to keep a confidence, and indeed should keep it, as long as no greater duty overrides.

One might argue that everyone has his or her own bailiwick, so to speak, and that priests, lawyers, and therapists are not police or prosecutors: it is not their job to accuse, try, or convict. But such an answer appears to us too easy, an expression of rule worship, or role worship, which upholds convention, tradition, law, or loyalty above principles of benevolence, nonmaleficence, and justice. We do not wish to ignore the importance of trust, but trust is not the only consideration in determining what is morally right or wrong, nor is it always an overriding consideration. The seal of the confessional, for example, even if thought to be absolute, cannot reasonably be so.

It is worth noting that, in these types of cases, the promise or duty of office is often used to protect persons guilty of fault. In the game of courtroom procedure, where attorneys are placed in an adversarial relationship, competing to see who will win or lose rather than cooperating in an effort to discover the truth, such rules appear to make sense. But, in morality, where truth may be more important than winning or losing, the rules of courtroom procedure should not override. Violating the law or a duty of office may have adverse legal consequences, damage a person's reputation, or cause financial loss, but these are consequences that must be taken into account in determining the morality of an act.

The question of *actual* right, we said, depends upon, among other things, *actual reliance* and not upon a prima facie right to rely. The question of actual right is a question that can be answered only after the fact, so to speak, when considering grounds for damages or claims. A court may want to know whether somebody had a right to rely, and this will depend, by and large, on whether that person actually *did* rely on a contract or promise of performance.

Consider the following case, taken from A. D. Woozley's response to P. S. Atiyah:

> If A, a land developer, publically declares his intention of building high quality houses on some land which he owns, and if he engages in subsequent conduct consistent with that plan, then B, who has never met A and owns adjacent land, may be justified in relying on A's going ahead with his plan and may financially commit himself to a project based on the expected rise in value of his own land. But A, if he drops his planned development, will incur neither moral nor legal liability for B's consequent loss. For that to happen B's justifiable reliance would at least have to have been induced by A's communicating to him about his plan. [11]

Woozley's point, it seems, is that there could be no legal or moral obligation to keep a promise, or to perform as contracted, unless a promise or contract was made, but there may have been justifiable reliance in the absence of either a promise or a contract. By "justifiable" here he obviously means "reasonable." Notice that a *right* to rely, on Woozley's view, does not arise, unless a promise, contract, or commitment is made *and is relied upon.* Thus, presumably, there may be good reason to rely even if there is no promise and no good reason to rely even when there is. The giving of an assurance *can* make a difference in determining whether or not there is a right to complain or seek compensation, and hence is not without moral or legal force. People should be held responsible for consciously creating reliance, and especially so, if we are correct, if they should not have created such reliance in the first place. They are responsible for preventing or mitigating the harm caused by their own intentional acts.

NOTES

1. Thomas Scanlon, "Promises and Practices," *Philosophy and Public Affairs* 19 (1990): 221.

2. Pall S. Ardal, "And That's a Promise," *Philosophical Quarterly* 18 (1968): 234.

3. Dennis M. Patterson, "The Value of a Promise," *Law and Philosphy* 11 (1992): 308.

4. Pall S. Ardal, "Promises and Reliance," *Dialogue* (Canada) 15 (1976): 55–56.

5. Ibid., pp. 55, 59.

6. David B. Seligman, "A Threat or a Promise," *Southern Journal of Philosophy* 33 (1995): 83–96.

7. Paul Ziff, *Epistemic Analysis: A Coherence Theory of Knowledge* (Dorecht: D. Reidel Publishing Company, 1984), p. 191.

8. A. D. Woozley, "Promises, Promises," *Mind* 90 (1981): 289.

9. Ardal, "And That's a Promise," pp. 230–231.

10. P. S. Atiyah, "Promises and the Law of Contract," *Mind* 88 (1979): 415.

11. Woozley, "Promises, Promises," p. 291.

eight

CONCLUDING POSTSCRIPT

W e have tried to show that the so-called practice of promising is plagued with a host of difficulties that render it incoherent, harmful, and immoral. We have argued that, generally speaking, people should not make promises and should not rely on them. Because promising is incoherent, it produces misunderstandings, creates unreasonable reliance, and causes unnecessary disappointment. People who take promises seriously must ignore other moral obligations, and people who take other obligations seriously cannot be counted on to keep their promises.

Accepted beliefs about promising lead people to think that they can create obligations just by claiming to have them, and such beliefs also allow them to think promisors can excuse themselves from such obligations for reasons that promisees need not accept. There is frequent disagreement about when or whether promises ought to be kept, and there is no accepted procedure for settling disputes. The promisor can decide that, despite giving assurance, he or she has no obligation, and the promisee is left with no clear remedy for the consequent loss, whether in the form of apology, restitution, or compensation. Promisors are exploited by promisees and promisees by promisors, for promising is by its very nature deceptive. It is often used to coerce or entice people to behave immorally. Promising is, indeed, a way of making immoral acts seem to be not only morally acceptable but morally obligatory.

Nevertheless, people do make promises and do rely on them. It is because of such reliance, we have maintained, that there can be an obligation of promise keeping, despite our claim that promise making is immoral. But keeping a promise is a defeasible obligation, and there are no generally accepted rules or procedures for determining when it does or does not hold. We believe, in fact, that promising is such a tangle of ambiguities that no such rules will stand close scrutiny. Thus, it is difficult and often impossible to confirm an obligation of promise keeping, just as it is difficult and often impossible to compensate for harms caused by promises that are broken. Justified promise breaking, we have pointed out, can be as harmful as unjustified promise breaking. A disappointed promisee may gain consolation from learning that a promisor has good reason for breaking a promise, but the harm is caused nonetheless.

This is not to say that people should never rely on one another. Reliance is important for many reasons, for people need to be able to count on others to do things they cannot do for themselves, and they need to be able to coordinate their actions with others to do the many things they cannot do alone. But there are many bases for predicting the actions of others, not dependent on promises, that do not create the same problems that promises do. Thus, the positive side of our story is that there are other, often better, bases for reliance than promising.

Indeed, we have tried to explain how contract law has changed over the years for the very sorts of reasons we have questioned promising. It has evolved from a promising model of contract to an application of statutes and legal principles, such as justice and nonmaleficence, in the adjudication of contract disputes, as contracts have come to be viewed, not as instruments of individualistic laissez-faire capitalism, but as instruments of social justice. Popular conceptions of promises have also changed in recent history, for people today seem to take promises less seriously than they did in the past and are less likely to rely on them.

But there is still confusion, even in contract law, about whether contracts really are or are not promises, and in ordinary life, about whether and when people are bound to keep their promises. There appears to be a great deal of tolerance for contradiction on this subject, because, apparently, people are not aware of the contradiction, or because it is only natural to want to have one's cake and eat it, too. People continue to believe that promises ought to be kept and yet allow that they may be broken for almost any reason. Not infrequently, they also expect more from others in the way of keeping promises than they do from themselves.

Such confusion has its price, however. Inconsistency in moral belief and practice can cause misunderstanding and conflict. Since contradictory beliefs cannot be reconciled, people sometimes act or judge one another according to the one belief and sometimes according to the other, frustrating themselves and one another. Believing that promises are assurances and also that they are not, they also believe that they can depend on them and that they cannot, having reason to believe in any particular case that a promise both holds and does not hold. Such confusion in fact creates the same kind of uncertainty about the future that promises are supposed to prevent, but under the illusion that uncertainty can be avoided, by assuring what cannot be assured. Such confusion supports skeptical attitudes regarding the objectivity of moral obligations. Since promising is founded on the idea that individuals can create obligations as they wish, it is just a short step to the belief that they can also cancel obligations, or simply ignore them, as they choose.

What, then, is a reasonable person to do? Well, to act reasonably, by not promising what cannot be assured, and by not relying on people who are not reliable. Morally good people, we have said, are generally not as reliable as people who take promises seriously and thus ignore other moral obligations. Morally good people will allow that other duties may override promises. Indeed, if fully aware of what they are doing, they will not make promises. If they can promise anything at all, it is only that they will uphold the moral law, whatever it requires. But they cannot promise even that, for if reasonable, they know that they are fallible and cannot really assure anyone that they will always do what they ought to do. What they will do is try to live according to moral principles and rules, according to their best knowledge and judgment, doing what others expect of them, or what they have led others to expect of them, if doing so turns out to be, in their estimation, a morally correct thing to do.

In dealing with others, we have said, a reasonable person does not make choices according to what he or she thinks others ought to do but on the basis of what he or she thinks they will do, or are likely to do. That is why reliance on promises does not depend on our belief that others have a duty to keep promises but on our reasonable expectation that they will. In any case, none of us can fully control others or the future. None of us can know for sure what will happen. Thus, for good moral reasons we need to stop trying to control the behavior of others by requiring them to perform in predetermined ways. Eliciting promises and holding people to their promises is one way of trying to exercise such control. Promising, or eliciting promises, may be rhetorically useful, but promises themselves are irrational, as Hume seems to have noticed, and hence should be excluded by moral law.

SOME IMPLICATIONS FOR MORAL THEORY

If our view of promising is correct, it has important consequences for moral theory. One of these consequences is that the supposed obligation to keep promises cannot be used as a paradigm of correct moral behavior, or as a test of the comprehensiveness or coherence of a moral theory. Promises do not, all by themselves, create obligations. It is the benefit or harm of keeping them that determines whether or not they are obligatory. Thus, a theory like act utilitarianism cannot rightly be criticized for claiming that promises ought to be kept only when promises produce utility. One might question the principle of utility, of course, but there is no good reason to criticize its application on the ground that promises create obligations. Whatever principles one accepts will determine whether and when promises ought to be kept. The supposed duty of promise keeping cannot override higher principles. Indeed, it is only by raising promise keeping to the level of a first principle, and the only and highest principle, that it may be thought to override all other considerations. But that is equivalent to holding that persons ought to keep their promises under any and all circumstances, which is absurd. If one allows promise keeping as a subordinate rule, as in social contract theory or rule utilitarianism, the same problems remain. A subordinate rule cannot be allowed to override first principles.

Genuine social contract theories face the additional problem of justifying the obligation creating force of the contract itself.[1] John Locke recognized this in arguing that the duty to keep promises or contracts must be more fundamental than the contract; in his view, it must hold in the state of nature.

> For it is not every compact, that puts an end to the state of nature between men, but only this one, of agreeing together mutually to enter into one community, and make one body politick; other promises and compacts men may make, one with another, and yet still be in the state of nature. The promises and bargains . . . are binding to them, tho' they are perfectly in a state of nature, in reference to one another. For truth, and keeping of faith, belong to men as men, and not as members of society.[2]

But, of course, social contract theories, like that of Rawls, really have little to do with contract: they are hypothetically based on principles or rules people would accept or agree to if they were rational. In a quasi-Kantian fashion, Rawls is simply asking what reasonable people should accept as universal laws, and this is hardly different from the question that all natural law and natural rights theories have raised. People should follow such laws, whatever they may be, not because they have agreed to accept them, but because they are rational. Talk of social contract seems misleading from the start.

The rules of society, including positive law, customs, and practices, may indeed depend on consent or acceptance, and perhaps even enforcement, but they do not depend on promises. The idea that all social rules presuppose at least implicit promises to accept and obey them is not only mistaken, it also raises the importance of promise making and promise keeping above all other considerations, making the promise keeping rule into a supreme moral principle. And, while the *actual* rules of society may require acceptance to make them actual, the *ideal* rules of morality, or the rules of reason, do not require such acceptance. The rules of morality, if indeed dictated by reason, must be independent of custom or practice. Conventional morality, or rules created by society by promising or acceptance, cannot define the limits of moral reasoning, or of moral rules and obligations, for such morality is itself always open to rational criticism. Promising certainly cannot establish moral rules if, as we have maintained, the making of promises is wrong to begin with, and if promises should not always be kept. These restrictions on promises presuppose the existence of higher principles and rules.

Is the view we are presenting not simply a reiteration of the arguments of act utilitarianism against deontology? Are we not saying that the morality of acts depends on consequences and consequences alone? Are we denying that the morality of future acts can be affected by actions in the past?

We have argued that the morality of keeping a promise in the future is not determined by the mere fact that a promise has been made in the past. In fact, we have argued that it cannot be so determined. But our point has been that the morality of keeping a promise cannot be determined by the fact of promising *alone*. On our view, promises *can* make a difference in determining the morality of an act. Promises can make a difference by creating reliance, and reliance can tip the balance in favor of creating an actual duty. However, other duties must be taken into consideration. So, to this extent, we have been in agreement with rule deontologists like Ross who speak of the duty to keep promises as a prima facie duty.

Unlike rule deontologists, however, we assume not only that there are other prima facie duties, but also that there are higher level principles that determine the morality of acts. In this respect, our position resembles Kantianism, or rule utilitarianism, except that we do not allow lower level rules to override higher level principles, as rule-utilitarians sometimes do. We have referred to the principles of beneficence and nonmaleficence which are, of course, presupposed by utilitarianism, but they are not peculiar to it. We have also insisted that each and every act must be judged on its own merits, but not independently of principles and rules, and not independently of consequences. Like objective utilitarians, we are also concerned about the actual benefit or harm caused by actions, and hence the actual benefit or harm of creating expectation, or of satisfying it, or failing to satisfy it, once created.

And, like utilitarianism, our argument is opposed to social contract theory, for our account of promises is meant to show that obligations cannot be created by promises or contracts without presupposing other moral principles or rules.

We have also been attacking philosophies of loyalty, honor, and trust, which hold that the obligation of promise keeping is so strong that it overrides all other considerations. Such philosophies exhibit, up to a point, the virtue of consistency, in holding that promises are genuine assurances, but they do so at the very high price of canceling the rest of morality—something which, upon reflection, they do not really want to do. They place a premium on keeping one's word, but it seems obvious to us that keeping one's word is not worth the sacrifice of other more important goods. Such a philosophy smacks of egotism, if not egoism, in being an expression of pride, inflexibility, and unreasonableness. It is, in fact, often used as an ego defense to cover, and at the same time justify, other faults. Loyalty to a person, group, or organization, expressed perhaps by an oath or a promise, is frequently a way of exhibiting bias or partiality. Organizations often demand loyalty from their members in order to protect the organization from criticism, or from litigation, by covering up wrongdoing, or by keeping it a secret. The purpose of such trust, therefore, is not to enforce morality but to subvert it.

Our thesis has been that promising is immoral. But our analysis of the problems involved in promising has also led us to point up how and why other theories have gone wrong. Indeed, our examination has called into question what many philosophers take to be the very foundation of morality itself—theories based on choice, commitment, loyalty, or trust. Throughout this investigation we ourselves have been motivated by the conviction that ethics is—or at least ought to be—an inquiry into the rational justification of human action; we have demonstrated, we believe, that philosophies founded upon promising are themselves irrational.

NOTES

1. See Michael H. Robins, "Promisory Obligations and Rawls's Contractarianism," *Analysis* 36 (1976): 190–98.

2. John Locke, *Two Treatises on Government*, "Of the State of Nature," chap. 2, p. 14.

BIBLIOGRAPHY

Altham, J. E. J. "Wicked Promises." In *Exercises in Analysis*. Edited by Ian Hacking. Cambridge, Cambridge University Press, 1985.

Aquinas, Thomas. *Summa Theologica*. In *Phiosophy in the Middle Ages*. Edited by A. Hyman and S. Walsh. Indianapolis: Hacket, 1973.

Ardal, Pall S. "And That's a Promise." *Philosophical Quarterly* 18 (1968).

———. "Promises and Reliance." *Dialogue* 15 (1976).

Atiyah, P. S. "Promises and the Law of Contract." *Mind* 88 (1979).

Baier, Annette. "Promises, Promises, Promises." Chapter 10 in *Postures of the Mind: Essays on Mind and Morals*. Minneapolis: University of Minnesota Press, 1985.

Bath, Katharine. "Promises and Assertions." *Philosophia* 8 (1978).

Bayles, Michael D. "Legally Enforceable Commitments." *Law and Philosophy* 4 (1985).

Cartwright, J. P. W. "An Evidentiary Theory of Promises." *Mind* 93 (1984).

Cavell, Stanly. *The Claim of Reason*. Oxford: The Clarendon Press, 1979.

Diggs, B. J. "Rules and Utilitarianism." *Philosophical Quarterly* 1 (1964).

Downie, R. S. "Three Accounts of Promising." *The Philosophical Quarterly* 35 (1985).

Feinman, Jay M. "The Significance of Contract Theory." *University of Cincinnati Law Review* 58 (1990).

Fox, R. M., and J. P. DeMarco, J. "The Immorality of Promising." *Journal of Value Inquiry* 27 (1993).

―――. "On Making and Keeping Promises." *Journal of Applied Ethics* 13, no. 2 (1996).

Fried, Charles. *Contract as Promise: A Theory of Contractual Obligation.* Cambridge: Harvard University Press, 1981.

Gert, Bernard. *Morality: A New Justification of the Moral Rules.* New York: Oxford University Press, 1988.

Gilmore, G. *The Death of Contract.* Columbus, Ohio: Ohio State University Press, 1974.

Hanfling, Oswald. "Promises, Games and Institutions." *Proceedings of the Aristotelian Society* 75 (1974–75).

Hare, R. M. "The Promising Game." *Revue Internationale de Philosophie* 18 (1964).

Hillman, Robert A. "The Crisis in Modern Contract Theory." *Texas Law Review* 67 (1988).

Hobbes, Thomas. *Leviathan,* pt. 1, chap. 14, para. 7.

Huizinga, J. *Homo Ludens.* London: Routledge and Kegan Paul, 1950.

Hume, David. "Of Morals," part 2, sect. 5, "Of The Obligation of Promises." In *A Treatise of Human Nature.* 2d. ed. Edited by P. H. Nidditch. (Oxford: The Clarendon Press, 1978).

Kading, Daniel. "On Promising without Moral Risk." *Philosophical Studies* 11 (1960).

Kant, Immanual. *Groundwork of the Metaphysic of Morals,* sect. 2.

Locke, John. "Of the State of Nature." In *Two Treatises on Government,* chap. 2, p. 14.

Macaulay, Stewart. "An Empirical View of Contract." *Wisconsin Law Review* (1985).

Macaulay, Stewart. "Elegant Models, Empirical Pictures, and the Complexities of Contract." *Law and Society Review* 11 (1977).

Macneil, Ian. *The New Social Contract (1980)*

McMahon, Christopher. "Promising and Coordination." *American Philosophical Quarterly* 2 (1989).

Mill, J. S. *Utilitarianism* (1861; reprint, Indianapolis: Hackett Publishing Company, 1979).

Mills, Jon K. "The Morality Promising Made in Good Faith." *Journal of Value Inquiry* 29 (1995).

Parfit, Derek. *Reasons and Persons.* Oxford: Clarendon Press, 1984.

Patterson, Dennis M. "The Value of a Promise." *Law and Philosphy* 11 (1992).

Pietroski, "Prima Facie Obligations, Ceteris Paribus Laws in Moral Theory." *Ethics* 103 (1993).

Posner, R. *Economic Analysis of Law.* Boston: Little, Brown, 1992.

Prichard, H. A. "Does Moral Philosophy Rest on a Mistake?" *Mind* 1912.

Rawls, John. *A Theory of Justice.* Cambridge, Mass.: Harvard University Press, 1971.

———. "Two Concepts of Rules." *Philosophical Review* 64 (1955).

Restatement of Contracts, 1932.

Restatement (Second) of Contracts, 1981.

Robins, Michael H. *Promising, Intending, and Moral Autonomy.* London: Cambridge University Press, 1984.

———. "Promisory Obligations and Rawls's Contractarianism." *Analysis* 36 (1976).

Ross, W. D. *The Right and the Good* (Oxford: Clarendon Press, 1930).

Sandel, Michael J. *Liberalism and the Limits of Justice.* New York: Cambridge University Press, 1982.

Scanlon, Thomas. "Promises and Practices." *Philosophy and Public Affairs* 19 (1990).

Searle, John. "How to Derive Ought from Is." *The Philosophical Review* 18 (1964).

Seligman, David B. "A Threat or a Promise." *Southern Journal of Philosophy* 33 (1995).

Sidgwick, Henry. *The Methods of Ethics.* 7th ed. London, 1907.

Smart, J. J. C. "Extreme and Restricted Utilitaraianism." *The Philosophical Quarterly* 6 (1956).

Smith, Holly. "A Paradox of Promising." *Philosophical Review* 106 (1997).

Snare, Frank. "The Definition of Prima Facie Duties." *The Philosophical Quarterly* 24 (1974).

Suits, B. "What is a Game?" *Philosophy of Science* 34 (1967).

Toulmin, Stephen. *The Place of Reason in Ethics.* 1950; reprint, Chicago: The University of Chicago Press, 1986.

Von Wright, Georg Henrik. "On Promises." In *Practical Reason: Philosophical Papers,* vol. 1. Ithaca, N.Y.: Cornell University Press, 1983.

Warnock, G. J. *The Object of Morality.* London: Methuen, 1971.

Wellman, Vincent A. "Conception of the Common Law: Reflections on a Theory of Contract." *University of Miami Law Review* 41 (1987).

Woozley, A. D. "Promises, Promises." *Mind* 90 (1981).

Ziff, Paul. *Epistemic Analysis: A Coherence Theory of Knowledge.* Dorecht: D. Reidel Publishing Company, 1984.

INDEX